ZEN PILOT

Praise for
Zen Pilot

"Robert DeLaurentis is a passionate pilot who is committed to sharing the magic of general aviation. His willingness to help others learn from his experiences, his focus on safety, and his excitement about flying make him both a valued member of the aviation community and a great example for anyone interested in discovering the fun, adventure, and freedom of flying."

—**Mark Baker**, President and CEO, Aircraft Owners and Pilots Association

"I've had the pleasure of meeting Robert DeLaurentis, "Zen Pilot", at aviation events where he has been a speaker. Having followed his solo circumnavigation flight in 2015, I have looked forward to the release of his book Zen Pilot which documents Robert's flying experiences during that voyage. What a great read!

Zen Pilot: Flight of Passion & the Journey Within *delivers Robert's amazing journey on so many levels. He is among the very few pilots who have pushed back the fears and mechanical concerns requested to undergo such an involved flying experience. You will learn what personal goals led up to his undertaking of such an 'impossibly big dream', the steps taken to accomplish it, and the hurdles he encountered (and overcame) along the way. The Zen Moments scattered* *throughout the book are great reminders to us about the power of being zen, especially in moments of stress and fear which are a common passengers when we take flight.*

While pilots will eat this story up, I believe anyone who aspires to reach higher and then live to tell it will thoroughly enjoy this 'hero's journey' adventure story that is as real as it can get."

—**Jack Pelton**, Chairman of the Board and CEO of the Experimental Aircraft Association and the former CEO of Cessna Aircraft Company

*"After reading **Zen Pilot** I can say I really like it! It's easy to read and I really like the 'Zen Moments' throughout the book. It's a good format because a person can pick it up at any point in the book and be engaged immediately. Both the experiences you write about and the writing of them are huge accomplishments. Good job!"*

—**Patty Wagstaff**, Aerobatic Champion & Airshow Pilot, Inductee National Aviation Hall of Fame

*"I just finished reading **Zen Pilot** and thoroughly loved it - this is REAL aviation at is best and I applaud your spirit of adventure. I particularly liked the "Zen Moments" as they are very insightful and will be beneficial to any pilot."*

—**Peter F. Bowers**, President, WACO Aircraft Corp.

*An innate part of human nature is to explore, to wonder what's on the other side of that ridge or to see a mountain and climb it. Robert DeLaurentis' book **Zen Pilot** demonstrates this quest for challenge, adventure and exploration and tells his story of circumnavigating the planet in his Piper Malibu Mirage. His first hand accounting enthusiastically keeps readers excited and challenged to reach for and realize their own dreams.*

Robert [or Zen Pilot], you don't just dream it, you do it!"

—**Dick Rutan**, Commander, Voyager Aircraft

*This book is a MUST read for any pilot or airplane-lover. From beginning to end Robert DeLaurentis wove a tapestry of sight, sound and Spirit with his writing. I just couldn't put it down. I particularly loved the Zen Moments interspersed in the book. We can all learn something about ourselves through reading **Zen Pilot**.*

—**Jolie Lucas**, Contributing Editor, ASN at AOPA: your freedom to fly, Opinion Leaders Blogger at AOPA; your freedom to fly and Founder, President at Friends of Oceano Airport

*"Sometimes we forget that flying is personal. The love for it we all share, but **Zen Pilot** is a reminder that the adventure of flight is as diverse as the people that take part in it. That the machines we fly can be our closest friends, yet moment later become teachers of some very tough lessons. That the world is*

so large that every landing strip opens a new patch of land, new people and new adventures to be had. You can question every pilot for who they are on the ground, but you cannot question their unique need to take to the skies and experience THEIR adventure. Robert did, and his story should at the very least be an inspiration to take on your own."

—**Jiri Marousek**, Chief Marketing Office / SVP of Marketing at AOPA

"All of us have dreams—some big, some small—of things we want to accomplish. In his book Zen Pilot: Flight of Passion and the Journey Within, Robert DeLaurentis reveals that his dream was rather big: to fly a single-engine airplane around the world. Alone. Whether or not you are a pilot, reading about his journey and how he got through some terrifying episodes is riveting. Like all big accomplishments, Robert's journey transformed him. Throughout the book, Robert outlines these transformative aspects of his journey, from conquering his fear, preparing for his trip, dealing with some big challenges, and ultimately breaking through and completing his big dream. His lessons, or Zen Moments, are peppered throughout the book, making it a great read for anyone who wants to accomplish their own big dream and transform themselves by doing it."

—**George A. Kounis**, Publisher/editor of Pilot Getaways magazine

ZEN PILOT

Flight of Passion
And the Journey Within

Robert DeLaurentis

Printed in the United States of America for Worldwide Distribution

ISBN-13: 978-0692787977
Library of Congress Control Number: 2017903800

Second Edition

Dedication

This book is dedicated to the spirit of adventure that burns inside each and every one of us. It lives deep in our hearts and souls, and when stoked and tended can become the burning passion that defines us.

Fearlessly pursuing this passion every day with the help and guidance of our higher power without regard for failure, ridicule or regret is our hero's journey.

To succeed on our journey requires us to go well beyond our limiting beliefs and our comfort zone, to go deeper inside ourselves than we ever thought possible.

In doing so, we open ourselves to what is available to us. This lightens us and sets us free of our earthly bounds. We then have the opportunity to inspire all those around us to embrace life and live more fully and completely.

Life is the grandest adventure of all. Each day is a blessing to be shared and embraced as we are "Flying Thru Life."

Special Thanks

I want to give special thanks to Susan Gilbert and Mary Marcdante. They have been and remain my two biggest supporters, guides and teachers on this planet. These two very spiritual women resonate at a higher frequency that lifts me when I am stuck, confused and frustrated.

There were times that they would point out that I wasn't being very "Zen." I pushed them to their absolute limits but they always stayed with me and supported me unconditionally and without judgment.

They offered up ideas or work that was nothing short of divine that left me speechless. Mary is an absolutely brilliant writer and editor, mindfulness coach and my constant cheerleader. She always saw the best in me even when I couldn't see it in myself. She could bring tears to my eyes with just a few words. She often speaks of hope, passion and what we are doing for the world.

Susan was the person who introduced me to my three life passions flying, small business and spirituality. She is my most trusted advisor and together we have been through so much. She has flown with me in Africa, Europe and the United States. She is my tactician and always has her eye on the big picture. When I wander off course she gently helps me correct. She created the structure, branding and social media that defines what it means to be "Flying Thru Life." Without her I would be lost in this lifetime.

Having Susan and Mary with me on this life journey has been one of my greatest honors and blessings. They have been and will remain my angels on the ground and in the air.

Contents

What is a Zen Pilot?

A Zen Pilot is someone who is Flying Thru Life and answering a call to adventure while inspiring others. Zen Pilots have a quiet confidence that comes from knowing that they are guided and are on their unique path pursuing their passions.

A Zen Pilot is brave enough to dream impossibly big and go after those dreams, accomplishing seemingly impossible tasks and goals with grace and ease.

A Zen Pilot is a way of being with oneself, others and the world that promotes open communication, gratitude, support and wonder.

A Zen Pilot applies insights gained from flying, travel, nature and silence to his or her daily life, especially for the benefit of others.

Prologue

Two-thirds of the way into my trip circum-navigating the globe, I looked at the altimeter and saw that I was climbing and passing ten thousand feet over the Strait of Malacca. The Strait is a narrow 435-nautical-mile stretch of water between the Malay Peninsula and the Indonesian island of Sumatra. Below me I could see a large number of merchant ships and, to the left, a dense jungle. Ships are always a welcome sight to pilots flying over open water. They offer a better chance for rescue should an aircraft go down. The recommended procedure is to fly across their bow to be sure someone sees you and then ditch your plane to either side to ensure you won't be run over—the turning radius of a ship is relatively big. All this awareness was normal and I was always taking note of my surroundings in case of an emergency because pilots know that things can change in an instant.

Glancing to my right, I saw the yellow oil-pressure warning light on the panel flicker! I gasped in an almost primal way as panic began to engulf my body. Oil is the lifeblood of an engine, and I had never once seen the oil light flicker in flight. This was not good at all.

About a second later the light went solid, the propeller instantly oversped up and the plane slowed as if someone had hit the emergency brakes hard. The oil that fed the propeller hub had been lost causing the propeller to abruptly go flat. Now instead of providing thrust, the propeller became a giant seven-foot rotating air brake. My stomach shot to my throat and my body slammed against my seatbelt straps. The engine shot beyond the redline, indicating the propeller was spinning at an impossible 2,750 rpm. I heard a deafening *errrrrr*, which meant that every part inside the engine was under great stress as well. It was as though it was saying, *Oh God, no! Please stop!*

The plane vibrated violently and it felt as if the entire engine was going to blow itself apart. I had never run my engine this fast and I was sure that it was doing serious damage with every critical second that passed. My 350-hp Piper Malibu Mirage was about to become a hot chunk of burning aluminum.

I was now rocketing toward the sea in an aircraft loaded six hundred pounds beyond its maximum landing weight limit with high-octane aviation fuel, just a foot behind me and to the right. Without power I had no way to stop it. All I could do was negotiate where the impact would happen.

My two worst fears as a pilot were occurring at the exact same moment in time: ENGINE OUT! SINGLE ENGINE PLANE OVER THE WATER!

My mind was racing. I might have to ditch in the ocean and I knew that meant my chances for survival were poor. Most likely I would be knocked out on impact with only one minute before the plane submerged. Sweat dripped down my back, and the smell of perspiration and fear engulfed me. This was what sheer and total terror and panic felt like. I had never really known either until now.

I had just joined a club that nobody wants to belong to. It wasn't just the engine-out club either. I had the engine out with 19.6 miles of water and jungle between me and the nearest airport in a foreign country known to have one of the worst aviation safety records in the world. Add to that, I was flying the equivalent of a bomb ninety extra gallons of fuel right next to me inside the cockpit with an ignition source (the high frequency radio and power supply) wired on top of it and separated by just a quarter-inch sheet of plywood. It's a miracle it didn't catch on fire.

Every minute I had spent studying aviation systems, principles, and emergency procedures; every minute of flight training; every word a flight instructor had ever spoken; every minute I had spent in the air; every article I had read … all of them were now going to be of use to me.

The Universe would not have it any other way.

Chapter 1

Flying Dreams

"The sky is blue-white above, and the blinding fire of the sun itself has burst over the ridge ahead….It's one of those moments when all the senses rise together, and realization snaps so acute and clear that seconds impress themselves with the strength of years on memory. It forms a picture with colors that will hold and lines that will stay sharp throughout the rest of life—the broad, sun-dazzled valley in the sky; the funnel's billowing walls; and deep down below, the hard, blue-gray scales of the ocean."

—Charles Lindbergh, *The Spirit of St. Louis*

As kids, many of us dream of flying. We stare up into the sky and know somehow that we were meant to make that part of our playground. My own passion for flying started at age six. As soon as I was able to draw, I was creating airplanes. I can remember making paper planes and flying them around the house and off the balcony. For me, driving in the car with the window down was an opportunity to imagine my hand was a wing and watch how it went up or down based on how I tilted it. Every time I heard a plane overhead I ran out to look. The sky was a place of wonder and fascination for me. Somehow I knew I had been there before. Whether it was as a bird, a bug or a pilot from a past life, the pull was undeniable.

My flying missions were, of course, limited to my imagination. I had flown countless sorties throughout my house with paper gliders and small plastic models I had put together. My creations always looked like they had been through a war or two, but in my imagination these aircraft took me many places. Sometimes I was flying over the Grand Canyon … other times I was flying inverted over Mount Everest in the fastest plane in the world.

As a child living in Jakarta, Indonesia, I got my first Cox string-controlled P-51 Mustang as a Christmas present from my parents. It looked just like a real P-51 Mustang, green with decals from WWII, an air scoop on the bottom, a bubble canopy and specially shaped wings that allowed it to fly inverted. While this was molded plastic stamped from a mechanical press, I was still thrilled beyond belief. I knew that with this plastic gas-powered model I would get a little bit closer to recognizing my dream of flight.

The plane had a device for the pilot's hand that when rotated up would pull a string that made the plane climb. By rotating the device down, it would pull the bottom string, bringing the model down as well. I could stand in the center of the circle and turn with the plane as it flew around me with my arm extended, rotating my wrist up and down.

A Cox string controlled P51 Mustang ready for its first sortie right out of the box.

After I had flown the P-51 on a few imaginary flights around the house, my Dad and I went to work testing the engine. We filled the small tank with the model-plane fuel that smelled like alcohol and oil mixed together, connected the battery to the glow plug engine and used the installed spring to spin the propeller.

Nothing.

Ah yes, we needed to prime the engine. We connected the spring to the leading edge of the propeller, turned it a couple times in the opposite direction to wind it up then … nothing. Okay, we needed to turn on the air fuel mixture screw. Then we got a burp from the little single-piston engine almost mocking us, *You Bozos have a lot to learn.* Undeterred, we continued. I was so excited I could barely stand still.

The little P-51 model engine would burp, sputter and spit fuel and exhaust for the next hour. Each time we tried to make it fly I felt as if I held all the hope a boy of six could possibly muster. But this dream of flight grew frustrating and as one hour turned into two, I could no longer hold my attention. I went into the house as my Dad kept at it. By what was likely the third hour, I had given up all hope and was onto a new project elsewhere in the house. Suddenly I heard a high-pitched sound like a hornet on steroids: Rheeeeeeee. I shot down the steps, made a turn toward the front of the house and there it was, running like it was ready to go to the moon! I was elated! If I could have hopped on that plane I would have ridden it into the heavens right there and then.

About five minutes later the engine ran out of fuel and stopped. It was smoking a bit and almost red hot, but what mattered was that it worked! In that moment I learned a lesson from my Dad that would serve me many times later in my life: Do not give up on pursuing my dreams. The things I wanted the most would cost me, sometimes dearly, but were worth pursuing.

Now my Dad and I wondered where we would launch this fire-breathing string-controlled beast. He came up with a plan to assemble lunch tables at my elementary school in Jakarta, Indonesia on the weekend when nobody was around to throw us out, so that our little model would become a navy plane lifting off from an aircraft carrier. I stood ready as my Dad worked his magic getting the plane started. After about fifteen minutes of sputtering and spilling model aviation fuel all over the table, the little engine sprang to life; the hornet was back and in action! Lines taut, legs shaking, I was ready for my first aviation adventure.

My Dad gave the little plane a push and it shot off, bouncing from table to table gaining speed, getting ready for liftoff. Unfortunately, the carrier runway was too short and the little model shot off the end of the last table and headed directly toward the ground. The hornet was silenced forever after the world's shortest flight.

In elementary school I built string-controlled planes out of balsa wood and, as a teen, radio-controlled planes that resulted in several unsuccessful flights. I crashed many of these simulated and real model planes but had great fun learning how planes worked and the aerodynamic principles that would later determine if I would live or die. But what was most important, these model planes lit a lifelong fire that would never end—flying!

It took me some thirty-five years to turn the dream of becoming a private pilot into a reality. The desire got stronger as time passed until it was no longer something I could deny. The military had told me no due to my eyesight despite my futile attempt to memorize the eye chart. My father directed me to accounting or business, something that would provide a safe and stable income for life. I followed his advice, but ironically, my business was so successful I was eventually able to cover the enormous expense of flight training and eventually flight. The call could be silenced for a time but not eliminated. That was my entelechy, when potential becomes realization and the blueprint for my life. It was God's intention for me in this life.

Zen Moment

As kids, many of us dream of flying. We stare up into the sky and know somehow that we were meant to make that part of our playground.

Zen Moment

In that moment I learned a lesson from my Dad that would serve me many times later in my life: Do not give up on pursuing my dreams. The things I wanted the most would cost me, sometimes dearly, but were worth pursuing.

Chapter 2

An Impossibly Big Dream

By anybody else's measure, I was living the American Dream. I had grown my real estate business to one hundred units. I had all the material comforts anyone could hope for. Yet, I had hit a wall taller than the highest thunderstorm I would face in my years of flying. I was holding myself back from the life that I wanted, and inside me was an emptiness I yearned to fill. My entelechy was nudging me, telling me that at forty-five years of age, I had less and less time to fulfill my life's true intentions.

One day, as I took my daily walk through Balboa Park, something changed. I had begun not to just notice the sights, sounds, and smells I had experienced on my previous walks, but to feel gratitude for them. I determined at that moment to begin my journey to bring purpose and passion into alignment with a higher power. I knew that if I had an impossibly big dream, the Universe would get behind me and partner with me. The resistance would fall away and things would start to flow, slowly at first and then at a feverish pitch. I quickly found that when I surrendered to what was for my higher good, the impossible would become the possible. I didn't know it at the time, but this was the seed planted that would grow into my dream of circumnavigating the globe in a solo flight.

In the next four years while completing an advanced degree in spiritual psychology with an emphasis in consciousness, health and healing, I was encouraged to have an impossibly big dream. By that time I had become a private pilot and had read an article about someone named Bob Gannon who had flown a plane around the world in the span of a year or two. My first idea was to fly across the

Atlantic. It seemed like the greatest adventure ever. After all, Lindbergh had done it.

I did it and when it was behind me, I realized that when I turned back from Europe I had gone almost half way around the world. I decided in a couple years I would do another trip and join all the pieces together. By now I had flown to Europe, Canada, Southern Africa, Mexico, Alaska and Central America. Why not do it all? Put the puzzle together.

I was asked countless times, "Why?" My answer was that it was my *impossibly big dream*. Flying a single-engine piston aircraft around the world was the greatest aviation challenge and adventure I could dream of and the hardest thing I could think of doing in my plane. It was the ultimate test of my flying skills as a pilot and would define me, stretch my limits, challenge me, test my mental strength and at times almost break me. My search for meaning would take me to the ends of the earth and over some of the most inhospitable terrain on the planet.

I also heard many voices of personal self-doubt. They would tell me that I was numb and trying to feel alive and that I was searching for meaning in my life. Before the trip it had been about making money, growing a business empire and letting my ego run wild. People sometimes described me as a hunter with conquest being my game. My former girlfriend, who often could see only the worst in me, was convinced I did it to be famous.

I had to admit to myself that I had spent a lifetime trying to get the recognition and attention of my father. Was I on some subconscious level doing increasingly daring and bold things to get the love I had always sought from him? He had taken me to the Tahoe Truckee Airport as a child to see the planes and the airshow. While he would never fly with me, I asked myself if I was living out his dream as well as my own.

I often felt a need to run away from life as if my soul had been restricted or caged. Flying, compounded with friends, travel and adventure was almost euphoric. Any one of these things would be enough to hold a person's attention but put them all together and it was off the charts. I think every soul secretly wants to return to the realm where it can move freely without the constraints of our human form. Flying gets us closer to that.

I worked for twenty-five years building a real estate business in San Diego. I had started in accounting at Arthur Andersen, and I well recall hearing a coworker tell about the money he had been making on a rental property he owned. He had time and extra resources that the rest of us did not have. My brother-in-law, who was playing golf or in his office strumming his guitar every time I visited, had an insurance agency and collected residuals on the policies he sold. Residual income— that was the answer I was looking for. I knew it the instant I saw it.

I wanted the lifestyle I saw in these two people. I craved that level of comfort and freedom from worry. I wanted my life to be more than what my father's had been. Up at 6 a.m. and home at 6 p.m., working himself tirelessly for some unthankful corporation that forgot about him although he had given his life to it. I felt that I had a greater purpose than to just run the hamster wheel of life and ambitions that would take money and time to reach. I wanted to change the world. I just didn't know how it would unfold. Nobody had an answer that would satisfy me … I would have to figure this out myself.

To make my future richer, I paid dearly by forgoing joy and happiness in the past. *I would never do that again*, I thought. I wondered what my life would be like now had I lived a more balanced life. Would I be married? Would I have a child? Or … would I now be setting out for the most ambitious journey of my life? My calling was this trip and it was pointless to live in the past and beat myself up in the present. And because I had sacrificed so much and couldn't change that, I decided to just enjoy the fruits of my labor. With few commitments with respect to family and relationships, I was as light as my plane and able to fly for very long times before my earthly commitments would bring me back to the ground.

This adventure I planned to embark on represented thirty years of hard work, determination, self-denial, dreaming impossibly big and working towards what seemed like an impossible goal.

In a naïve way, I thought this trip around the world would be similar to my trip from San Diego to Sardinia, Italy, two years before. My goal on that trip was to cross the Atlantic to Europe in a fashion similar to Lindbergh's. I never expected to go much farther than Stornoway, Scotland, but once I got there I realized that everything in Europe was geographically close and an hour- to two-hour flight could get me to the next country. On this trip I would joyfully get to fly through Northern Africa, the Middle East, Asia, and Australia. I mean how much harder could it really be? I had just crossed the Atlantic.

I was totally wrong.

Zen Moment

I quickly found that when I surrendered to what was for my higher good, the impossible would become the possible.

Zen Moment

Every soul secretly wants to return to the realm where it can move freely without the constraints of our human form. Flying gets us closer to that.

Chapter 3

Becoming the
Spirit of San Diego

The plane that would eventually become the *Spirit of San Diego* was an eighteen-year-old 1997 Piper Malibu Mirage. I bought her three years before with about fourteen hundred flight hours, which is quite low for any aircraft. I paid $360,000 and she would undergo a remarkable transformation in avionics (electronic systems) from that point forward. And her build and details made her more than up for the long-distance flights I had in mind.

This was a sexy aircraft on the ramp and in the air with high performance to match. To me she was the "Divine Feminine" in all her glory and I loved her unconditionally. Her wings were very long and thin, like legs on a supermodel. At forty-three feet, the wingspan was longer than many entry-level jets. The fuselage or torso was long, thin and muscular like a professional dancer. The surfaces were smooth and the rivets sunken and almost invisible to reduce the wind resistance, which gave her a flawless skin. That combined with the nano-ceramic coating by Flight Shield made her look as if she were somehow made from one sheet of slippery liquid metal.

The Piper Malibu Mirage that would become the "The Spirit of San Diego" prior to extensive modification and upgrades for her historic circumnavigation of the planet.

Like a jet, the cabin was laid out in cabin-class comfort, which meant that the back four seats faced one another, making the cabin more social and providing an opportunity to spread out comfortably. She was intended to fly high and fast but carry only a couple of people with bags and, when fully loaded, 150 gallons of fuel. More of a high-altitude sports car than a hauler, she was about as close to a jet as you could come with a piston engine. In fact this model was often converted into a jet-powered aircraft because she was able to handle the speed and power of a Pratt & Whitney turbine engine.

The cowling that covered the engine was made long to house the forward storage compartment as well as the engine. It made her look as if she had a mile of engine up front. The exhaust vents were closely mounted to the cowling as if she had a small, delicate and symmetrically shaped nose. The propeller was all business and a work of art at the same time—four blades, MT composite scimitar and nickel tipped. You just knew that designers had spent weeks at a supercomputer hammering out the most aerodynamic angles and dimensions possible. It looked like four sword blades had been intentionally used to slice through the air. I often saw that people couldn't resist putting their hands on the propeller, no doubt attracted by the danger it represented when the engine was operating but also its sheer beauty when it was static.

The Piper Malibu Mirage had an up-sloping rear tail section that defied gravity. Nimble and strong but not an ounce more that she needed to be to get the job done … she was memorable. There was indeed something special about her. She was elegant, sophisticated, intelligent, physically and mentally strong, adventurous and above all else *fearless.* One look at her and you knew this was a serious airplane, one that wasn't playing games.

With a high frequency (HF) radio whose antenna went out the pilot side window to the left wingtip and then back to the tail, she had bionic ears and voice, which could keep me in contact with air traffic controllers out to one thousand-plus nautical miles. She could fly as high as twenty-five thousand feet and into known icing conditions. I was told in an emergency I could take her up to twenty-eight thousand, assuming the turbo chargers didn't get too hot. The plane had twin turbochargers and retractable landing gear, which made her fast at altitude and the long wings with extended range tanks made her capable of flying very long distances. Add the attachable ferry tanks and no country or continent was out of range.

High maintenance

The problem was that when you extract every ounce of performance that is humanly possible from an aircraft and piston engine you are going to wear it out quickly; it will be subject to failures and need a large amount of maintenance. This was a tradeoff I was willing to pay. With such complex systems this airplane was never designed to be a workhorse or to be abused. It was, as one instructor called it, a "fire-breathing dragon." The normal cruise speed was close to 230 mph, an impressive performance from any piston plane. She was high maintenance but high performance as well. She had been pushed to her material limits to achieve this performance, most of her parts engineered for that and not for durability.

I often wondered what the Wright brothers, Lindbergh or Amelia Earhart would think if they were flying next to me. I am sure they would be proud to fly this aircraft and would be in awe of its modern-day technology.

The plane was equipped with radar and a storm scope as well as the older six-pack of steam gauges, which include an altitude indicator, altimeter, turn coordinator, airspeed indicator, compass and a vertical speed gauge. The first round of improvements included many upgrades: a glass cockpit Primary Flight Display (PFD); satellite radio and weather; synthetic vision (which showed the topography of the entire earth); active traffic to see other planes up to thirty miles out; new communication and navigation radios; touch screen GPS with a large display; and GPS steering, which allowed me to program an entire route of a trip from wheels up to about two hundred feet over the destination runway regardless of the visibility.

I made a decision to stay with the older steam gauges (not really powered by steam but a joking reference to the antiquated technology of the day) on the copilot side. This meant that in the event that my higher tech left side had issues, which it occasionally did, I could revert to the lower-tech steam gauges on the right. The other advantage was that the older gauges were in circulation throughout the world, making replacements easy to find or be repaired. Not being integrated into one unit also made it possible to replace the gauges independently without complicated equipment or extensive training. It was the right combination of technology, reliability and common sense.

The value of a plane is determined by the value of the avionics and the remaining hours left on the engine. Everything else was free according to one old timer. (*For a complete description of the plane's innovations, see Appendix One.*)

What's in a name?

I wanted to create a strong connection to the great people of San Diego to help them feel part of the journey and to get excited about it. I pondered about this for days, but I wasn't coming up with something that would accomplish the goal.

Eventually I asked the Universe for guidance with respect to this great adventure. It was clearly getting bigger than me, and I could use the help. The connection point I needed came to me one morning as I woke from a deep sleep. It felt as if the words had been placed magically on my lips; all I had to do was move them and I spoke the words in a soft whisper as if they were meant just for me to hear: The "Spirit of San Diego."

This moment had divine energy, and I was quite aware that I was being guided and this was the path that I was intended to travel. It was also strategic, a way of branding the plane and my work for greater impact locally and globally. We did a trademark search and filed the application, a process that takes six months and is subject to anyone's filing an objection. We found that a ship in San Diego had the same name, but fortunately for us, it was never trademarked. Having the name the *Spirit of San Diego* for the airplane would make this trip timeless, something that would be forever tied to the city. Its fame began to grow.

The "Spirit of San Diego" the day before her departure from Landmark Aviation in San Diego adorned with the 23 flags of the countries she would visit on her circumnavigation.

The city would go on to establish a "Spirit of San Diego Day" that would log information about the trip in the history books. The plane, which was becoming a sought-after attraction, was part of the Parade of Planes in Palm Springs at the Aviation Expo and was also part of static displays at various other air shows.

For my personal message, I wanted to somehow link my three passions: flying, spirituality and business. The plane would clearly be the vehicle that delivered it to the world.

To further tie Lindbergh's flight to my own, we decided the following:

1. I would also cross the Atlantic solo.
2. My departure from the continent would be on May 20 as was his, eighty-eight years earlier, in 1927.
3. I would also leave North America at St John's, Newfoundland.
4. The *Spirit of San Diego* would have some of the most innovative technology of the day, as did Lindbergh's plane.
5. Many companies from all over the US contributed to the effort with systems that

were assembled, modified, designed, and installed here in San Diego. Lindbergh's plane, the *Spirit of St. Louis*, was built here in San Diego. Ryan Aeronautical built the plane, and his Wright Whirlwind engine was built by Wright Aeronautical of New Jersey; the magnetic compass came from another state as well. Both were cutting edge for their day.

6. I would be leaving from San Diego's Lindbergh Field, where Lindbergh first field-tested his famous plane in preparation for his flight.

The *Spirit of San Diego* had many more technological advantages, of course. Indeed it showcased innovative technologies that had been designed, engineered, manufactured, assembled or installed in San Diego. These innovations served to improve climb performance and make the plane faster, more fuel efficient and—perhaps most important—safer.

Naming her the *Spirit of San Diego* meant that I carried the hopes, dreams, heart, and spirit of

San Diego with me on this historic flight. This call to adventure showcased San Diego, aviation technology, raised money for charitable causes, and showed people what is possible with training, good decision making and the right equipment. This plane represented the very best that San Diego had to offer.

Ferry configuration and "showboating"

In order for the *Spirit of San Diego* to go the distance of approximately twenty-six thousand miles, it would need several modifications. Many of the legs would exceed her published range of 1,423 nautical miles in economy cruise. This meant the plane would need a ferry system—attaching temporary fuel tanks that would enable the plane to fly greater distances. For this I went to Fred Sorenson of Flight Contract Services, a legend among pilots who had even a thought about ferrying an aircraft from one place to another. Being with Fred, you knew you were in the company of a special professional. Not only had Fred been in an Indiana

Jones movie, piloting Indiana to safety from a pursuing group of angry spear-throwing and arrow-shooting natives, his character was on the hit TV series Family Guy, and he eventually became a Lego action figure.

It had taken me more than a year to get my plane ready for her first North Atlantic crossing. Now, for an around-the-world flight, I would need yet another year to really get to know her. You were always waiting for the surprises that you missed. So I wondered, *How is Fred alive considering that the two most recent ferry/circumnavigation-attempt pilots I know of died on their first attempts at Pacific Crossings?* Fred had over five hundred Pacific crossings in planes that he barely knew. Statistically that was impossible to explain.

I asked Fred, "How are you alive?"

He responded in his usual calm, brief way, "I know when not to go, and if I go, I know when to turn back." That explanation didn't satisfy me. I knew Fred was around for a reason. For a second I thought it was to help these people transition. To usher them out of this physical world. To help them complete their contracts with the Universe. Fred knew the enormous risks these people were taking even if they didn't, so he teaches to help others understand and mitigate the risks.

It was like taking up a profession in Russian roulette and surviving well into your sixties or seventies. I was not able to answer the question during the course of that trip aside to say that we were both meant to be around well after the trip to share something more. Fred was one part grim reaper and one part pure angel.

Before taking me on as a client, Fred had a conversation with me that I often refer to as the "No showboating" talk. He was extremely clear that he didn't want me to put the trip all over social media and turn it into a circus. The ferry process that allows planes to travel vast distances was intended to get aircraft to distant locations not intended to support adventure seekers in their desire to circumnavigate the world. Fred felt using the ferry system in this way would make the FAA unhappy.

The FAA didn't want the liability or publicity related to an adventure trip that could result in a potentially catastrophic situation.

The no-showboating conversation was, for me, a dilemma. My intention was always to do positive things for general aviation and to get the word out; this was in direct conflict with Fred's intention, which was solely to get me around the world safely and quietly. I knew that, frankly, some drama would amplify and extend my message. I quickly found out that people wanted to share in the wins on my trip, but most people found the very nature of it so absolutely terrifying that they went instantly into worry mode when anything went wrong. And on a trip like this there was no doubt that some things were going to go wrong, people would worry and the drama would heighten.

I never resolved this conflict with Fred. He would later mention to me that he was not going to continue to support the around-the-world flights for record seekers and adventurers. I wondered if I had done these future pilots a service or disservice.

Zen Moment

Eventually I asked the Universe for guidance with respect to this great adventure. It was clearly getting bigger than me and I could use the help. The connection point I needed came to me one morning as I woke from a deep sleep.

Chapter 4

Overcoming Fear of Flying

On previous flights, I remember during night flights over the Indian and Atlantic oceans looking at the empty copilot seat in the low eerie glow of the instrument panel and thinking, *You are very much alone in this.* Later I came to realize that fear filled that seat and would be riding with me every nautical mile of the trip. Trying to get rid of it would prove futile. It was strapped in just as snug as I was and I couldn't kill it off. Fear would be my unyielding companion for some twenty-six thousand nautical miles, and would at times take me over, control me and run unchecked throughout every inch of my body. Fear was a demon that would at times make me doubt everything I believed about myself and my skills.

Fear would remind me that relaxing for just a minute could be the end of this journey, and me. You are only as good as what you are doing right now, it would say. The Universe does not give you a pass on anything. You must be perfect or suffer the consequences. The Universe can be cruel and it doesn't always follow a set of rules.

Over the next several months I would learn that fear would play a large part in my life.

Throughout the six months of preparations I did for this flight, family and friends contacted me to air their concerns about the risks I was taking. Many of my followers on social media seemed compelled to share their version of what could happen to me. Among those who begged me to cancel were my father, a close friend, and a former girlfriend who told me in graphic detail about her dream that I died a terrible death in the open ocean. I reminded myself that these were people who cared for me, but their fears were not my fears.

I did not need to take these on. The dreams represented what I refer to as "False Evidence Appearing Real" or FEAR. I also knew from my spiritual psychology studies that death in a dream oftentimes meant rebirth.

My plate was full with my own fears. I decided that the risks I would be taking were ones I was willing to take. I decided I would rather pursue my passions and fail miserably than to ignore them.

That being said, I could get on with dealing with my fear. And as a pilot who flies over oceans, deserts, mountains and other "inhospitable terrain" on a regular basis, I'm well versed on this topic. Over the years, I've learned there are a number of ways to help get past these fears and live a more adventurous and fearless life.

One technique I used to overcome my fear was to break the risk down into the smallest pieces and mitigate them individually. Here is how I coped with it:

The support of a trusted team

I assembled an amazing team to support me, including Fred Sorenson and Eddie Gould, from General Aviation Support Egypt (GASE), my trip manager. Eddie was like the Great Oz. He is a Brit, both brilliant and experienced, having guided others on their circumnavigation and ferry flights. Never far from his computer and his cigarettes, he was awake almost every minute I was in the air, watching out for my interests. Motivated by his love of aviation, he was an invaluable asset and dealt with anything that came up whether a need for a part, a permit or the best lodging to be found for fifty miles. Clearly one of my angels given to me to guide, encourage and listen to me share my overwhelming frustration and stress, Eddie helped me through some of the most frustrating moments in my life.

Equally important for the successful completion of my trip was finding the right mechanic. The relationship between a pilot and his mechanic or mechanics is critical. It would not be an overstatement to say the mechanic has the power of life and death over any plane or pilot. It's a relationship that must be nurtured and developed. For pilots, finding an expert you can trust 100 percent may be one of the most important things you can do to help ensure your survival.

My plane was painstakingly examined at two of the best repair facilities in Southern California: High Performance Aircraft in El Cajon and Advanced Aircraft Service in San Diego. I had entrusted my safety to both these repair facilities many times. Before the trip they made an intensive investigation of the inside of the cylinders, tested the oil for signs of metal and of course checked the compression in each cylinder to name a few.

Experience from having successfully completed these long-distance flights also taught me that having multiple mechanics at different shops was essential. The issues that seemed to perplex one shop were glaringly obvious to the other. One of my mechanics specialized in the Piper products while the other was more a generalist. Having specific knowledge was always useful but then a mechanic who worked with other planes had the benefit of that experience as well. Additionally, depending on the size of the shop you might find that the senior mechanic in a smaller shop might be spending more time on your plane, which had its benefits as well.

I also reminded myself of the "invisible team" that would help guide me. Air traffic control systems cover large portions of the globe. Air traffic controllers map and monitor the airways and virtually all of them speak English. Minimum safe altitudes are clearly defined in addition to myriad approach and departure procedures that generally ensure a safe arrival and departure throughout the world.

Experience makes a difference

Quite simply the more we do something the easier it becomes. Furthermore, most of the things we fear don't happen. I reminded myself that this was not my first rodeo: I had flown myself successfully to thirty countries in the last three years.

Flying the dirt strips in isolated parts of southern Africa where the terrain was designated "inhospitable" and the rivers were filled with crocodiles made this trip seem manageable in comparison.

Use available technology

Amelia Earhart never had GPS satellite technology as part of her plane's avionics panel. Not to mention that we now have the iPad and iPhone, which are remarkably capable backups and I've used them to navigate north of the Arctic Circle! Add to that, Garmin traffic systems that give pilots a comprehensive traffic picture, terrain avoidance, onboard radar, a lightning strike finder, satellite technology to download weather information and digital flight charts with synthetic vision that creates three-dimensional environments that you fly through and covers every inch of the planet. Technology today is truly remarkable.

Training, training, training

Let's not forget the obvious. Success ultimately comes down to having the ability to handle whatever situations the Universe presents. During the most challenging parts of my trip I intentionally was alone because I didn't want to subject anyone else to this risk. I was comfortable with risk because I had been flying my plane for five years and was intimately familiar with all its systems.

I practiced my emergency procedures over and over again. Emergency depressurization, engine out, smoke in the cabin and electrical failure until I had it covered. I was at the top of my game when I departed.

My greatest fear on this trip is what would happen if I needed to ditch in the open ocean. The good news was that statistics indicate that 95 percent of people survive the water impact. My plane had airbags installed to improve my chances on impact, and I had memorized the emergency procedures.

To handle the real challenges that would come after the impact, I took an open ocean survival class with Corporate Air Parts. There I got into a pool to practice open ocean survival skills, and to become familiar with the challenges of inflating a life raft and getting in.

Don't scrimp on survival gear

The survival gear I carried with me on my trip weighed about forty pounds. During my flight I wore my neoprene survival suit, which I not so affectionately referred to as my "Gumby suit." It smelled like perspiration and rubber and was designed to cover the entire body from head to toe and form a tight seal around the face. Imagine a red ping pong ball floating on the water getting kicked around by waves for hours on end while taking in an occasional mouthful of saltwater, with God only knows what swimming around you.

I also had packed items including a life raft, lighted life preservers, dye packets, fishing gear and a knife and an ax to cut my way out of my seat belts and the plane if necessary. My plane had an onboard satellite locator beacon and I wore another one around my neck. The survival bag had backup handheld marine and aviation radios as well as a satellite phone. Additionally, I was required to carry several million dollars in survival insurance; I had evacuation and medical insurance as well.

It was difficult to carry all that I needed since I would be flying over all types of terrain including deserts, mountains, frozen tundra and water. My complete gear was packaged neatly together in one bright yellow bag and in a way that ensured it would float. This way I could toss it out the plane in one motion and it wouldn't weigh me down if I needed to swim to the life raft or shore. The bright color of the bag would also help others spot me if I ditched the aircraft.

My Survival Gear

Six-person life raft yellow compass (2)   Flashlight

Fishhooks   Sewing needle

Signal mirror (2)   Survival candle

Emergency blanket   Goggles

Self-sealing waterproof pouch   Poncho

Potable water purification technology   Sunglasses

Rescue strobe with flashlight   Laser flair

Fire starter sticks   Toilet tissue

Safety light sticks (2)   Pocketknife

AA Batteries   Lighted life jackets

Delorme inReach Explorer   Floating PLB

Emergency sleeping bag (2)   Water

Food   Sat phone

Bright orange ball caps   Flint

Emergency blanket   Razor

Tube tent   Utility cord

Ax   First Aid Kit

Waterproof matches   Wire saw

Leader line and sinkers   Whistle

Backup aviation and marine handheld radios

Think of everything

My list was extensive and included everything from having Garrett Neal from Neal Aviation check the operation of my avionics, to checking that I had the proper visas for all the countries that required them. It was so detailed that one item included checking to ensure the plane's registration documents had the expiration dates clearly marked on the copies. This mistake a couple years before had gotten my plane impounded by Panamanian officials and delayed my departure from Panama City by almost a day. This was after an interrogation by the senior attorney of the Aviation Ministry who was trying to drive the Fixed Based Operator (FBO) out of business so he could take over.

The final details of my preparation bordered on extreme paranoia. I had flown this trip several times in my head already and thought through the entire aircraft to see if there was anything I didn't need and could remove. I was gravely concerned about the amount of weight I was asking the plane to carry. I remembered in Charles Lindbergh's book,

The Spirit of Saint Louis, how he described in order to keep the weight down he removed the top part of his flight charts for terrain he would not be flying over. I was going to do everything possible to learn from Lindbergh's adventure.

I spent an hour in Target looking for the absolute smallest, lightest binder and dividers to hold my travel documents; I counted out exactly ninety of each of my vitamins and placed them in plastic bags. I figured that the extreme heat of the Middle East would melt or burst the fish oil capsules so I put them in a separate plastic bag. I remember actually pausing to decide if I wanted to take the risk they wouldn't burst so that I could save the weight of one plastic bag. In my final attempt to reduce weight I removed all credit cards I didn't anticipate using from my wallet. The cost of carrying anything I didn't need all the way around the world was enormous in terms of money and weight. Every ounce would matter when I would be taking off and asking more from the *Spirit of San Diego* than I ever had before.

I was now as prepared as I thought I could be. My plane appeared to be mechanically perfect. I had a backup for all critical systems including GPS, flight instruments, fuel, oil and communications. The one glaring weakness and risk was that I was flying with only one engine.

It was a major risk I could not mitigate.

However, while some would swear having more engines is safer, Charles Lindbergh pointed out that a second engine is just another one that can fail. Such potential issues as fuel contamination and volcanic ash affect all engines simultaneously meaning that in those cases there is no advantage to having an additional one. To add to the challenge, flying a twin-engine plane with one engine is extremely difficult due to the asymmetrical thrust that is put on the plane and the fact that twin-engine aircraft can't maintain high cruising altitudes on one engine. If you were over a mountain range it was just a matter of when you were going down not if.

No matter how much planning I did, I knew my last leg—the Pacific Ocean—would be the most challenging. It was the longest and, with the additional fuel I would need, I would be flying the *Spirit of San Diego* at her heaviest weight. I would worry about this leg the entire trip because no matter how many legs I completed, the hardest last leg was before me. Though my skill level would naturally increase during the course of the trip, the cumulative fatigue would get worse, kind of like the stress a student feels as he gets closer and closer to the day of the final exam.

The Pacific was the final test of my determination, metal, courage, and one of the greatest battles of my life. It was *vast*, the biggest of all the oceans, immense, beautiful, unforgiving and often deadly. As one of my social media naysayers reminded me before I left, "The Pacific is littered with planes that didn't make it, including that of Amelia Earhart."

Sponsors

As I gave the *Spirit of San Diego* a final inspection the day before takeoff, I thought about the additional stress I carried with me related to my sponsors and everything I had promised them: social media coverage; mention on TV, radio and newspapers; a chapter in my book; (*See Appendix 2*) mentions in my speaking presentation slides. Their multicolored logos lined both sides of the aircraft and the wingtips. I referred to the plane with its many logos as a circus when I saw it on the graphic designer's computer. I had agonized whether to grey over the logos so they wouldn't stand out so much— so it wouldn't feel like a circus. A few of my friends thought it would be "blasphemy" to mess with a sponsor's logo. Another thought the plane would look "prettier" with the colors muted to keep from clashing with the plane's color scheme. Conflicting information, as was typical in aviation.

I ultimately went with the circus—mostly because everyone knows when the circus rolls into town. I wanted maximum visibility and I didn't want to have to apologize to even one sponsor for something that happened on this trip. I wondered if they had thought about how it would reflect on them if something went wrong. Terribly wrong. Many had made the decision to sponsor me with little contemplation; it was more a spontaneous thing without thinking of possible consequences.

I wondered if it would have been better to be anonymous as on my previous trips north of the Arctic Circle and over the North Atlantic from San Diego to Sardinia. On those trips I could really focus on the flying. But for this trip, I had decided to go bigger. A little attention, I thought, would be welcome. Yet, I was not used to being the center of so much attention; I was unsure how that would feel and how I would handle it. I was also concerned about negative comments that would surely pop up. Was associating my flight with Lindbergh's going to excite people or would I be seen as some guy trying to be more than he was?

I didn't want to be the guy who selfishly checked the boxes for myself and then talked about them later. My desire was to share what I had learned about the passion of flight and my message, to look beyond myself and to give back. This felt right and I accepted that this was the direction in which I was being guided. No need to resist it. I would go with it and see where it took me. I was learning that this was what surrender felt like. I felt confused, frustrated and, at times, a little out of control and scared. Growth came in spurts. I needed to be patient; when the time was right things would happen as they were intended.

By the time I left I had prepared for everything I could anticipate. It was the things that I could not anticipate that were concerning me. What could the Universe have in store for me? I knew there would certainly be something.

Zen Moment

It was time to look beyond myself and give back. I knew this was the direction in which I was being guided. No need to resist it. I was learning this was what surrender felt like.

Chapter 5

Day of Departure

The day of departure from San Diego dawned sunny, bright, and full of enormous anticipation. The past months of planning and what felt like a lifetime of hard work had led me to this moment in time. It was my impossibly big dream wrapped up into the most epic flying adventure I could imagine.

As much as I thought I had prepared for this trip, the small voices in my head kept asking, *What are you doing? You have no idea what you are in for … You might not be coming back … You should have listened to your family and friends.* The voices of self-doubt that lived inside my head were active, and I knew them well. They were terrified and wanted to keep me small. This was the worst time possible time for them to speak up.

What really frightened me on this day was that this time I knew the voices were right. This was going to be one hellish and challenging chapter in my life that would test me to my very limits. Limits I couldn't define and certainly some I didn't even know I had. I was praying that this wouldn't be the end of my life and that I would return to San Diego. That I would see these people again who were sending me off on this journey to some of the most remote places on the planet where people didn't care about me or my dreams. I had no way to anticipate what sort of chances I was taking, and I honestly didn't know if I would be coming home. At a minimum, I would not return the same person as I was when I left ... in a way I was saying goodbye to myself as well.

In the next three months, despite all I had done to mitigate and banish my old friend Fear before this trip, it would return and be with me every step, every turn and every frustrating dead end along the way. Fear was the doubter, the coward, the one with the bad attitude, the one unwilling to take a chance for something better that lived inside each and every one of us. Fear was desperately trying to save itself in this life-and-death struggle. Begging me to turn around and say, "Sorry folks not today, I don't have what it takes and this was a gigantic mistake." Fear would bring out the very best in me and at other times the very worst. It would also be one of my greatest teachers.

I reminded myself that fear was not me. Not even close. I felt I was on the verge of something big and I wasn't going to give up. I wasn't going to let fear take control of me and turn me into a zombie that was half alive and half dead. I was committed, but I had my demons to battle once again. They were lining up in front of me, row after row as far as I could see. We had fought many times before. It was never fun, pleasant or without spilled blood and broken bones. It was always a close fight and sometimes difficult to predict the outcome. I had won many times before and lost a few, but I knew that this was a fight worth fighting. I wanted to know that I could take on impossibly big challenges and achieve them. It was about self-respect, honoring my word, defining myself by love not fear, continuing on my journey, spiritual evolution and believing in myself even when those closest to me could not see past their considerable overwhelming and incapacitating fears.

This was a union with my angels, a test of my faith on a scale I had not experienced before. I was reminded that the Universe doesn't distinguish between big and small so I might as well ask for it all. "All" would include a fantastic trip to twenty-three countries, five continents and crossing more than twelve oceans and seas, meeting many wonderful people, improving my flying skills, seeing the planet in all its unbounded glory, getting to do what I loved, which was flying, expanding my world, raising money for my charities, and above all else, having one hell of a good time.

The faith I'm referring to would not be what I had known before. I believed that something bigger than me existed out there somewhere, but now I believed I would be dependent on this something to get me home to my family and friends. That the determination of one man was not enough to take on the challenges that were headed my way. The world was too vast, the oceans too big and the weather too strong for me to take alone. For this trip to come to a successful completion, for me to declare victory, I would need the assistance of everyone and everything, divine assistance included. In fact, at my most challenging moments, terrified and seemingly hopeless moments, I would directly ask for assistance. For this epic trip I was open to all possibilities it would take us all working together.

Media attention

My digital marketing PR team had crafted and released an amazing press release the day before my departure. We hoped the sendoff would have reporters from major TV channels, newspapers and radio stations. Surprisingly, the media was nowhere to be seen. We learned that there had been a death across town that journalists were eager to cover, an indication of the media reporter's need for what got them good ratings. The only death at Lindbergh Field that morning was the dead silence as I looked across the tarmac. I would get to know that silence intimately over the next 150 hours of flight time.

If the media had the ability to read the future, reporters would have been all over my story. I thought about how things were unfolding perfectly, as they were intended ... I just didn't know what that was. Perhaps it was the calm before the hellish storm? Most people can meditate for about ten to fifteen minutes. I was about to experience what would seem like a lifetime of peace and quiet punctuated by "moments" that would define my life.

At this point I decided to put my energy into receiving what was available to me rather than trying to figure all this out. This was an entirely different approach to living, but I would quickly find that there was a pool of information and assistance I had no idea that existed to me as a pilot. It was the "collective conscious." It contained all the wisdom of everyone who ever lived. All I needed to do was tap into it in my times of need, sort of like logging onto Google to ask a question. I knew the hard reality ahead would help me with this and much more. If ever I wanted an opportunity to overcome the issues that blocked me, this would be the time they would be presented to me to work on and potentially release.

What I was struggling with was why I was so damn uneasy? My stomach was in knots and in the silence, I was concerned that someone might actually realize how utterly and completely scared I was… Would they see past the bravado, would they see me as the real deal or just another yahoo off to get some attention that he never got as a kid?

I was sure that by the end of the trip the very best and worst of me would surface. I didn't even know what either of those were, but I was pretty sure it would be clear by the end of the journey. Did I really want to go that deep? Or would I be happier, more content on the shallower side of life?

Most people live there and seem to be satisfied with that for their entire lives. Why should mine be any different? So many unanswered questions.

Takeoff!

The "Spirit of San Diego" in all her glory the day of her departure from Landmark Aviation at Lindbergh Field.

Despite my lingering fears, the images that remain from my departure day tell a different story. The video and photos taken at Lindbergh Field show a picture-perfect San Diego day with glorious sunshine, lots of smiles and a clean and shiny plane that seemed ready in every way for the journey ahead. (See http://bit.ly/zen-pilot-departs) If she were to speak, the *Spirit of San Diego* would say that she could do this, that she was strong and able to take on what the Universe could throw her way. She would speak of optimism, good intentions and positive energy. With total confidence in me, she was unaware that I doubted myself.

It was a serene moment filled with encouraging words about "going for it," "achieving your goals," "making history" and "inspiring others." All that was starting to feel like a lot of extra responsibility to carry on my shoulders. Had Lindbergh heard the same sort of thing before he took off? I looked up toward the heavens, which would be my home for the next ninety-eight days. Would it be heaven for me … or hell?

I did my run-up for the last time before my journey began. I was parked just off the departure end of Runway 27 (Magnetic heading 270). I went through my checklist. GPS in heading mode on the autopilot, parking brake on, fuel on fullest tank, check flight instruments for correct readings, rudder trim set to E, run up engine to 2,000 rpm, check magnetos (shutting off one and ensuring the engine was still running then switching to the other), check alternators (shutting off one and ensuring the engine was still running and then switching to the other), vacuum pump in the green, ice protection check, throttle at idle check, seatbelts tight, flaps at 10 degrees for takeoff, defrost on, oil temp to 160, pressurization set for cruise altitude, pitot heat on, doors locked, fuel mixture leaned, prop full, flight director set, transponder code set, traffic screen at ten nautical miles. Everything seemed perfect. I was ready for takeoff!

I called ground control and let them know my run-up was complete. They instructed me to taxi to the runway hold short line and contact the tower and notify them I was ready for instrument flight rules (IFR) release. This means that the plane is flown with only reference to the flight instruments oftentimes in zero visibility weather.

My hands fit neatly into the yoke and I lightly pressed the mic button and in my most confident voice: "Tower, N997MA holding short Runway 27 ready for IFR release." I let out a deep sigh of relief after I released the mic button. *That came out well*, I thought. The next thing I would hear was that I was cleared to enter the active runway and start my ground roll.

A Southwest 737 lined up in front of me and slowly spooled up its enormous turbofan engines, a giant in comparison to the *Spirit of San Diego*. The big jet's engines whirled and whined and started to create enormous thrust right in front of me. I thought how each of those engines was one hundred times more reliable than what I was flying. How comforting it would be at this moment to know I had Rolls-Royce reliability powering the *Spirit of San Diego*. As the thrust grew the roar of the engines became deafening, but the sound soon became more distant, replaced by the sound of my pounding heart.

Then the voice from the tower: "N997MA, cleared for IFR release Runway 27 caution wake turbulence 737 departing."

The "Spirit of San Diego" taxiing behind the bigger, more capable and vastly more reliable Boeing 737, trusting that she was up for any challenge that was presented.

I slowly increased the throttle and released the brakes to pull onto the runway. I waited a bit to let the wing tip vortices settle after the 737 lifted off. I wasn't in a hurry. I could see the 9,400 feet of asphalt that lay ahead of me and twenty-six thousand nautical miles beyond that, which would get me back to this same spot three months and eight days later. I was almost breathless thinking about all that must happen perfectly to get me back safely. If ever there was a moment of truth it was now.

By this time my heart was ready to pound right out of my chest. I had this sense of doom and excitement that I was just about to pull on the tail of the tiger. I was also not sure I had ever been this scared.

I did my "Lights, camera, action" checks: landing, pulse, strobe and position lights were on; the transponder code that identified me on the air traffic controllers screen was entered correctly; and then I gradually applied full throttle, fuel and propeller rpm. As the engine came to life, the sound was so loud that even my Lightspeed PFX noise-cancelling headset could not totally silence it. I released the brakes and the plane lunged forward like a racehorse out of the gates.

Six months of long hours, hundreds of calls to sponsors, details, visas, plane modifications, frustration, more frustration, maintenance, training, blogging, branding, public relations, fear, overcoming obstacles and dreaming were behind me. I was truly living in the present and would remember this moment for the rest of my life. I wondered if this had just been a fantastic dream and now was the time I would wake up.

"Airspeed alive," I called out.

In my mind I could hear the voice of my flight instructor Bill Orland telling me, "Engine instruments green…"

Fifty knots: "… apply right rudder, stay on that centerline…"

Sixty-five knots: "… pull back on the yoke and protect that nose wheel" (the most delicate part of the aircraft)

Eighty knots: Lots of runway ahead, the plane was accelerating nicely at this configuration of 10 percent over max gross weight.

Eighty-five knots: Here I would normally rotate with 10 degrees of flaps, but I wanted to build up some additional speed because I was heavy. I could feel the vibration of the tires on the runway.

One hundred knots: I was flying … lighter than air … lifted from my earthly bounds.

Zen Moment

Facing these challenges was about self-respect, honoring my word, defining myself by love not fear, continuing on my journey, spiritual evolution and believing in myself even when those closest to me could not see past their considerable overwhelming and incapacitating fears.

Zen Moment

The Universe doesn't distinguish between big and small so I might as well ask for it all.

Chapter 6

In Flight Emergency

I was now flying just as I had dreamed about so many times as a little boy. Then in my dreams I would just put my arms out and will myself into the air. It was the best feeling and something I always knew I could do. I was born to fly.

I was told later that from the ground, the takeoff seemed like a moment of total peace and serenity, all inspiring music and fairy dust. In the cockpit it was anything but a "Zen" moment.

At four hundred feet above the runway my landing gear failed to properly retract. I was dragging my nose wheel. The engine—a 350-hp Lycoming twin turbocharged one—was at full horse-power trying to deal with the extra weight of the ninety gallons and 540 pounds of extra fuel I was carrying.

I knew my gear had failed to retract because only two of three landing gear indicator lights showed gear fully retracted. The gear warning light was fully illuminated in bright orange. The Universe had just sent me my first challenge, and I wasn't even four hundred feet off the ground! I could hear the extra ninety gallons of high-octane Avgas just inches behind me sloshing around in the ferry tank. No way could I go back and land at this weight; the landing gear could not support it and would more than likely collapse as I touched down. I was a flying *bomb* at this point! A deep sense of doom and dread overwhelmed me. How could I make it to twenty-three countries with landing gear that didn't work?

"Gear Warning" light indicating a gear failure on takeoff marking the first inflight emergency of the trip.

The day before I had flown the plane to Lindbergh Field to position it for departure and a warning light showed itself as well. I got the gear down and called the mechanic to make some adjustments on the plane. He did the work, but we both knew to fix the problem 100 percent would require a more complex and time-consuming effort to put the plane up on jacks and swing the landing gear. This would of course delay the departure. This decision felt out of character based on the detailed planning and attention to detail I had demonstrated so far and it would be the first mistake I would make on the trip. It was motivated by my desire to keep to my schedule, or a fatal flaw that most pilots exhibit at some time in their flying careers described as "Get-There-Itis." The Universe would quickly give me feedback on my decision to proceed.

The plane was flying slower than it normally would in that configuration, which confirmed for me that the wheel was dragging. Returning to the airport I just had left would have been a public relations nightmare; it made sense to continue on my trip and burn off the fuel load I was carrying. I had the good sense to make the first leg one of the longest figuring I could ferret out any problems that might develop with the plane. In Muncie, Indiana, where I planned to land, I had access to a Piper Authorized facility that would make repairs for me if necessary.

Now I had about eight hours to figure out how to fix the problem and plenty of time to plan for a potential gear-up landing on my first leg. If I couldn't find a solution this was going to be one of the shortest circumnavigation attempts of the world ever.

I decided to first try to cycle the landing gear down and then up at altitude, once I reached cruise at twenty-one thousand feet and everything settled down.

I was feeling panicked and alone, wondering if the Universe was testing to see if I was strong enough or stupid enough to do this trip. Then, as if in surround sound, I heard the voices in my head say what I can't stand to hear: "The Universe has the power to take you out any time it wants. Are you sure you are up for this?" I definitively was being warned, but at the same time I felt the angels were on my side, watching over me. My plane glowed and its energy felt very special. As I look back I don't think it is possible for anyone to do this trip and survive the countless challenges without some form of divine guidance and support. It was just too complicated, too dangerous and too hard.

A landing gear nightmare

When I did cycle the landing gear, I set in motion a complex series of events driven by the "sequencing valve." This involves the gear doors opening, the nose wheel dropping out of the compartment and then rotating 90 degrees, where it then locks into place. The right and left "mains," or main landing gear, open outward and the landing gear doors are directly connected to the landing gear structure. This operation often resets the landing gear, but I got yet another surprise. After the fifteen-second whine of the hydraulic motor that operated at 1,500 psi and the sequential clunking of the landing gear like someone was hitting the bottom of the plane with a sledgehammer everything came to silence. It was like standing in front of a slot machine watching the lights, spinning wheels, listening to the sounds and waiting for the outcome— would you be a big winner or loser? In this case, though, the outcome could determine if I would live or die. I got only one green this time, and then nothing more. I was looking for three green lights.

My problem now appeared to be worse. I had the right main landing gear that was now down in addition to my first problem: the nose gear not retracting. I was flying at 21,000 feet with no ability to land the plane. The reality of this was beginning to hit me. Gear up landing first leg. Distance traveled: 1,600 nautical miles. Countries visited: zero, plane totaled injuries to be determined.

At the time all this was going on, I was catching a ride on the jet stream blowing west to east across the US. It was giving me a near 45-mph push from behind, but due to my landing gear dragging, I was making only my normal cruise speed of 190 knots. (A knot is equal to 1.15 mph.) I made the decision that when I got to my destination I would fly by the tower and ask if the gear was down. But the Universe had something else in mind. By the time I arrived in Muncie, some eight-plus hours later, it was dark; no one in the tower could see the plane well enough to tell me. Alone with this problem, I was overcome with a sense of doom.

I did what any pilot would do, which was to start going through the emergency checklist. I pulled back on the yoke, which made the nose of the plane quickly move upward to create a down force hoping the weight of the gear would pull it down. This is similar to going up in an elevator; you feel heavier as the elevator starts to move. I was intentionally pulling Gs, and slowing my speed so the spring that pushed the nose wheel down could apply pressure against the force of the oncoming wind. I pushed the rudder left and right frantically trying to get the gear down.

While I was frantically trying to get the landing gear in place for landing, there was a circus going off in my head. The voices were shouting at me by now: "Look what you got yourself into! You didn't make it very far! You didn't plan for this!" Suddenly the third landing light went on, showing that the nose wheel and landing gear mains were now in position and locked for landing as I turned from my base leg to final approach. From my dry lips and mouth, I thanked God; I and my aircraft had made it. It felt that permission had been granted to continue on this trip—if I dared.

I had a perfect landing. It was gentle as the mains touched down and then the nose, and I was reminded that landing is when your soul reconnects with the earth. Landing is in fact an art form and no pilot can do it perfectly every time. Too many factors come into play: condition of the runway, other aircraft, turbulence, wind, airspeed, and of course the pilot's state of mind. I was so thankful that the gear had done its job, but I worried if this was a foreshadowing of things to come. The experience had taught me that my perception of my plane as perfect was neither true nor possible. No machine can be that. It is just a matter of time until something fails. I closed my eyes that night feeling tired and confused and praying for an easier flight the next day.

When I arrived at the airport the next morning, I found my plane up on jacks at the hanger. An old timer named Don, who had been repairing Piper landing gears for years, was working on mine. I commented how complicated the landing gear system was and he promptly disagreed. Don then launched into excruciating detail about the operation of the hydraulic actuators and the sequencing valve and how the front tire rotated as it retracted into the plane. I knew then I had the right man for the job and with him had just overcome the first hurdle the Universe had thrown my way.

I pulled myself back into the moment and next leg that I needed to complete. If I could somehow continue to put these legs together one by one I would eventually make it home.

Zen Moment

I was feeling panicked and alone, wondering if the Universe was testing to see if I was strong enough or stupid enough to do this trip. Then, as if in surround sound, I heard the voices in my head say what I can't stand to hear: "The Universe has the power to take you out any time it wants. Are you sure you are up for this?" I definitely was being warned, but at the same time I felt the angels were on my side, watching over me.

Chapter 7

Threading the Needle

Within thirty minutes Don had completed tuning the landing gear and it was back to operating perfectly. I was greatly relieved and sure that I would no longer have to deal with the gear on this trip. Still, if I could have taken Don along on my trip, it would have been a comfort. Clearly I was fantasizing at this point … it was time to get back to reality.

The second leg would take me from Muncie, Indiana, to Bangor, Maine. Flying just south of Lake Erie I came into some of the most challenging weather I faced while traversing the US. It surprised me that my worst weather would be here at home when I was going to be crossing distant and foreboding parts of the globe. I had assumed that the planet would put together ever-bigger challenges over vast oceans of the world, or while flying by Everest or perhaps the deserts of the Middle East. This was simply not the case for me.

Playground in the sky

The beauty that I experienced on my trip was almost incomprehensible at times. I never got tired of flying in and around the billowing white fluffy clouds. In fact at times I felt like I had quite a love affair going with them. They were each unique and magical and often times went as far as my eye could see and then my imagination beyond that. The clouds were limitless and reminded me that I was quite small when compared with the vastness of them. Their scale was of course enormous, sometimes reaching up to sixty thousand feet, more than double the altitude that my tiny plane could fly.

I was in a three-dimensional fantasy world with giant cotton ball-shaped clouds that could form into countless different shapes. They were alive with energy, water and of course Spirit. One day I would see a giant dog with droopy ears and another day it was an ice cream cone with three scoops of vanilla ice cream. Whatever my imagination could dream up, I could find it. I was like a little boy given these enormous puffy white play toys that I could reach out and touch with the tips of my wings. Or when I was inspired, I could hide inside them and pop my head up to see as far as the eye could see. In reality, it was a vast ocean of pure life-giving water that spanned the entire planet. It was my playground in the sky.

Sometimes, I would imagine the clouds as a three-dimensional obstacle course and fly narrowly between vast formations. I would raise my wing to avoid a cloud, pretending they were in fact solid and that I would lose my wingtip should I touch them. Other times, I would set the aircraft altitude and just skim the very top of a cloud layer with only my head above the clouds. It was like I was slicing mile-long strips of whipped cream with a razor-sharp forty-three-foot-long white wing. The plane was clearly an extension of me. I was the soul and the plane was my heart and body.

I was twenty-one thousand feet above the earth and in heaven as far as the little boy in me could see. Strapped into the plane I had dreamed about as a little boy. What child has not imagined being inside the cockpit of that model plane doing loops, rolls and dives while making the sounds that aircraft do? Thinking, *Wouldn't it be fun to fly through the clouds? Vroooom, Swiiiiiish.*

The very same clouds that could provide such joy and exhilaration to my inner child could also in an instant rip and tear my fragile plane apart. The Malibu Mirage had a long documented history of in-flight breakups. The forty-three-foot thin wings were known to snap if the plane wandered into an imbedded thunderstorm.

Mother Nature clearly called the shots and I knew her moods could change very quickly from the playful loving friend to tempest. And when Mother Nature is angry she cares for no man or plane. Thankfully she often reveals her fury with dark and different shapes that can give us the tipoff. She always held the upper hand and was a force so strong that my relationship with her was second only to that with my plane. I was there with her permission and I knew that weather was clearly one of the greatest threats to my safety.

Thunderstorms can hold hundreds of thousands of pounds of water and have enough force to lift this water over sixty thousand feet into the air. An airplane weighing 4,300 pounds is like a feather in the air and inconsequential in comparison. I was quite aware that when compounded, the over-gross situation due to the extra fuel carried on most of the trip and flight speeds of 230 mph, created a potentially dangerous situation when confronted with any significant weather.

Deciphering weather

With respect to weather, I was responsible for all decisions. It would have been ideal to have a daily weather brief from a professional, but that was available only in the US and Canada. This meant I had to get weather information from multiple sources. I filed most of my flight plans each evening for the next leg using software from Rocket-Route.com, which put together briefing packets for my route when the information was available.

However, in some parts of the world the weather maps did not relate to the area I was crossing, making it critical for me to find other sources of weather information. One source were the "handlers" that airport regulations sometimes required me to use. Handlers were people or companies that had negotiated the rights to assist pilots that landed at their airport. These handlers could charge whatever they wanted and often charged bogus fees to line their pockets, though the functions they performed could—if truth be told—be done by the pilots themselves. The handlers would help file flight plans, provide weather briefs, walk pilots through customs and immigration, help with bags, fueling, and move pilots around large airports that might not be friendly to small aircraft or foreigners.

In some places like Brisbane, Australia for example, handlers were happy to take your money and fail to provide service. There I was told that the brief was the pilot's responsibility. At first I explained that we all needed to work together to keep pilots safe, but it took several more forceful requests on my part to actually get what I had paid for. At Brisbane one handler told me that it was okay to use automobile oil in my plane since they didn't carry the type I needed. Doing so could have caused catastrophic damage to the *Spirit of San Diego*.

I also got weather information off moving maps on Jeppesen and Garmin Pilot software when it was available and I had an Internet signal. A reliable source was www.aviationweather.gov. It covered a lot of the globe and, because it came from the US, I had some confidence in it. I always had my backup plan, which was Eddie Gould of GASE; I was able to contact him for weather info on the ground and in the air via satellite text and email. Eddie is a technical wizard on his computer when he had an Internet signal in Egypt and he was always willing to do whatever he could to help.

Certain regions of the world such as Malaysia have regional weather reporting that pilots can access. For the most part I did so by talking to local pilots and flying clubs, which I found to be enormously helpful.

The weather information I received from these sources didn't always, or even often, agree, but I was at least put on alert if one of the sources anticipated bad weather. Doing most of my flying by day, starting around 10:00 a.m. when I was fresh, allowed me to see large developments of bad weather and do what I could to avoid it. NEXRAD satellite weather ended at the midway point in Canada forcing me to use my onboard radar; surprisingly it never really seemed to match what I saw out my window.

This conflict was of great concern to me, but it was only when I got back to the US that I noticed tucked away in the upper-right of the display screen the words "Stab Inop" or stabilization inoperative. This meant that the radar could not maintain focus on the same point on the horizon if the plane was climbing or descending. It would seem higher as the plane was going up or lower if it was going down. This would explain why I got so little useful information from the radar during the trip. Similarly, my on-board strike finder never displayed a single lightning strike during the three months and eight days. This was clearly an indication that it was not working based on the volume of weather I experienced on my trip. As I reflect back on this lack of weather information I began to feel that on my trip I wasn't much better off than Lindbergh with respect to onboard weather. In fact, I was at times worse off since the information I believed to be correct was not.

I recall a text response I got from fellow earthrounder named Matt Guthmiller when I inquired what weather site he used. He said that he found most of the weather info worthless once he got into Asia because the different weather reporting services forecast towering cumulous clouds and thunderstorms every day. So you would either park your plane and not fly for the next two months or deal with it. He was right. Flying without reliable weather reporting around the world was a chilling point to consider.

Dealing with weather issues seemed much more personal and intimate in a small airplane like the Malibu Mirage. While it is a capable aircraft, there was no denying that it was minuscule compared to the larger and safer commercial planes that most people fly. These planes were designed to be flown every day for many years and hundreds of thousands of hours. Nobody had even broken the ten thousand-hour mark in a Malibu Mirage. Often times it felt like I was being tossed around in the air like a ping pong ball. The risk was real and always present.

Onward to Maine

As I continued the leg that would take me to Bangor, I had towering cumulous on both sides. Air traffic controllers were directing me to the right or left of the weather, but my first thought was to go over the top of the storm front. It was developing quickly and my intuition told me to stay clear since the Malibu had a reputation for breaking up in flight when they wandered into storm clouds. The wing had been strengthened in model year 1998, the year after my plane was built, but that couldn't change the fact that the plane had a forty-three-foot wingspan. It's like supporting a large weight in the middle of a long stick—too much stress and something has to give.

Eventually I would thread the needle in a fairly dramatic fashion between the two dangerous storm clouds. This was a bit like walking between two tigers; either one could swallow you up if you got close enough.

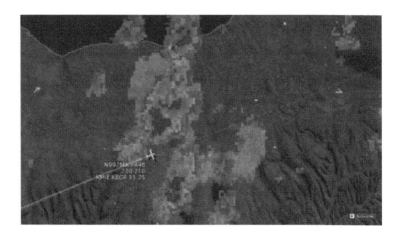

The "Spirit of San Diego" threading the needle between two
thunderstorms enrounte to Bangor, Maine on the second leg of the trip.

Flying a metal object next to or into a lightning storm would obviously put me in danger of a strike, which made threading the storm even more crucial. Equally terrifying was that dense precipitation could force a plane down in a violent fashion or drown the engine by taking in too much water. These storms offered no dividend apart from the drama they represented to the crowd that was following on social media. For me, they were a very real reminder that the weather was like spinning a roulette wheel and losing was a distinct possibility.

It is never recommended that you pass closer than twenty miles from one of these storms, but in this situation I did not have that luxury. I tightened my seatbelt as tight as I could get it, but I knew from past experiences that when the turbulence was extreme, my head would hit the top of the plane due to my height. It was never enough to knock me out but it was always startling and painful as I was lifted out of my seat.

I bent over in my seat with my teeth clenched, anticipating imminent head knock with roof of the plane. The plane began to shake and bounce violently, kind of like a bad amusement park ride except you are doing it at over 200 mph. In my head I was listening for the music that always comes with the ride but it never happened. And as quickly as it started it was over. I was expecting much worse as I transited this choke point in the clouds.

Zen Moment

I was twenty-one thousand feet above the earth and in heaven as far as the little boy in me could see.

Strapped into the plane I had dreamed about as a little boy. What child has not imagined being inside the cockpit of that model plane doing loops rolls and dives while making the sounds that aircraft do? Thinking, Wouldn't it be fun to fly through the clouds? *Vroooom, Swiiiiiish.*

Chapter 8

In Foreign Territory

Flying in Canada and Europe was relatively easy. Portugal, Spain, Switzerland and Malta were great places to visit and some of most enjoyable stops I made. I was hopeful the rest of the trip would be this easy, but I knew that was a fantasy. Although I had no idea what was to come, I knew it wouldn't be this comfortable.

The island of Elba, just off the west coast of Italy, was, like St. Moritz, Switzerland, an airport that had a visual-flight-rules-only (VFR) approach due to the extreme difficulty of the terrain. The down-sloping runway at Marina di Campo had the ocean on its south side and mountains packed right against it on the north. The airport had published two charts to help pilots navigate the terrain, but they really showed how insane the approach truly was. First you had to line up the 195-degree radial that led you to the airport. Once you were established on this inbound course, it took you between a couple of mountains and then you would turn 35 degrees to the left at the last minute to line up on Runway 16.

What made the approach even crazier was that it required descending at a rate of 10.2 degrees, which is three times steeper than the usual decent rate of 3 degrees. And then the worst part of the approach: clearing a 508-foot-high mountaintop by just sixty-six feet. If any winds were present they would accelerate over the top of the mountain and create a down force, which would slam a plane into the front side of the mountain.

The tower operator cleared me to land. He said with a heavy Italian accent, "Noveember Nieener Nieener Seben Mike Alfa, Buon Giorno! Clear to land, on-a six, weind on-a 16 knots."

With a 10-knot headwind I had exactly the down force I was trying to avoid. In a slow and aerodynamically "dirty" landing configuration, the *Spirit of San Diego* can drop like a rock with the nose pointed dramatically down so I was able to achieve the 10.2-degree descent angle, but I was not willing to get that close to the mountain top. My personal minimum is closer to two hundred feet; needless to say, I was too high and way too fast for the short runway of Elba.

As I crammed the throttle forward to forty-three inches of manifold pressure, the 350-horsepower Lycoming twin turbocharged aluminum aircraft engine thundered! *Berrrm!* The aircraft responded quickly as I was light on fuel and at sea level. Every naked Italian on the beach below me got a "*Buon giorno* from America," and they will never forget the *Spirit of San Diego*. The sound must have been deafening and bounced around the bay as I overflew the runway at three hundred feet. I was almost immediately over the beach and then the water. In order to make it back to the airport, I would have to turn hard to the right and hug the shore and then almost immediately turn the opposite direction to the hard left to clear a point that projected out on the bay.

As I was putting the *Spirit of San Diego* through her Italian gymnastic routine I realized I had cut things a little too close and didn't need to do the air show for the locals. I could have headed straight out to sea and done a much slower and less dramatic course reversal. As I cleared the point, I knew I had the runway made and had just given everyone a free peek at the bottom side of the plane that was covered with black oil that had been blown over the last few legs. I completed my turn, lined up on Runway 34 and floated down for the end of another successful and adrenaline-filled leg. I always thanked the *Spirit of San Diego* at the completion of every leg for getting me to my destination safely. She had been put through her paces and performed well.

On this day, I learned that I could not trust the foreign approach charts that the pilots use for landing. In this case the approach plates put me too close to mountains, didn't take into account dangerous downdrafts and required extreme descents. They could potentially put me into dangerous situations that were beyond the performance capabilities of my plane. Losing faith in approach plates reminded me that there were few certainties on my trip. I was being tested on a daily basis and learning from each challenge that came my way.

Air traffic controller standoff

I was about one hundred nautical miles from Corlu, which is about 100 kilometers west of Istanbul when I came upon a storm front. It didn't look that bad as initially I could see beneath it, but I had a nagging feeling in my stomach. Something wasn't right. I knew I needed to do something about it. So I lit off the radar.

I didn't get much of a return, but as I got closer the storm started to look darker and darker below it. I had the resources of time and fuel, which meant I had no reason to take any risks. To get away from the storm, I asked Istanbul approach for a vector 25 degrees to the right, which was granted. But the air-traffic controller wasn't happy about it in that I was going twenty miles off my course and that put me close to a Military Operations Area (MOA).

In the next fifteen minutes the air-traffic controller requested three times that I return to my original course and three times I told him "No," that I could not comply due to weather. He became more and more insistent and I became more and more insistent. I wasn't going into that storm!

Saying no to authority figures, in particular air-traffic controllers, when things are happening quickly is something that pilots don't often do. But by this time I was very clear on my intuition. I was definitely correct and I was being guided. With time, I made my way around the storm and had been handed off to Istanbul radar, probably the busiest frequency I have ever been on.

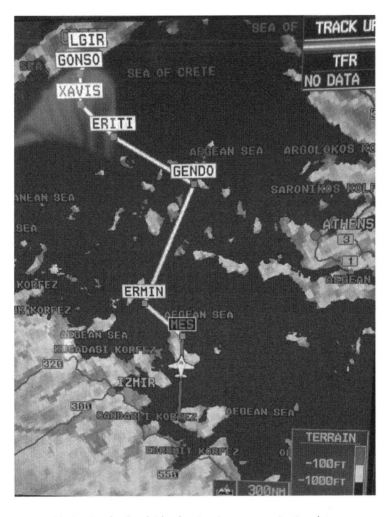

Navigating the Greek Islands using Jeppesen navigation data

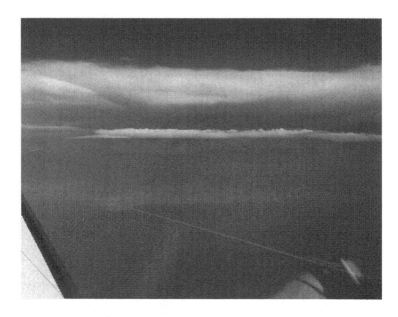

Approaching Istanbul, refusing to enter a storm front as directed by
air traffic controllers.

The controller seemed to be speaking
without taking a breath. He was rattling off tail
numbers and shifting planes to other frequencies
like bullets out of an Uzi. I made four attempts to
communicate with him and I was totally ignored. By
that time, I was getting close to the airport and I
was still at eighteen thousand feet. I was starting to
panic and absolutely insistent that he talk to me at
this critical point in my flight.

I keyed my microphone to block all his communications with all other aircraft in flight and told him that I needed a response. After being ignored for what seemed like an eternity, I was making myself his number one priority above all other flights. I explained that I was going to stay on his circuit until he handed me off or gave me the descent that I requested. I said, "Istanbul control, N997MA is making my fifth request to begin my descent. I am over your airspace at eighteen thousand and need a response. I will continue to use your circuit until you acknowledge me."

I took away his ability to use the circuit, letting him know I had control if he didn't deal with me. As I held the mic for an extra second I knew this would have seemed like an eternity to anybody on the radio. I was unsure what the response would be in this foreign country and my heart started to beat faster. Had I overstepped my bounds? Would they ground me? Impound my plane? Fine me?

Having the courage to do a flight like this meant that I was not afraid to be bold, but I also knew I was taking a calculated risk and this clever maneuver could have some severe and unpredictable consequences. At that point, the air-traffic controller came on and in an agitated voice gave me the descent to altitude I had requested. I was the squeaky wheel and my plan had worked.

When I got on the ground, I fought with the ground crew to find out what they would charge me for fuel. Having resolved that and just after I completed the fueling, the storm front I had been avoiding came through with all the force Mother Nature could muster. It went on for twenty-five minutes and dumped ungodly amounts of water. I could barely see ten feet in front of me.

I watched in terror, knowing that I had avoided a tragic event that would have certainly taken me out. I breathed a deep sigh of relief knowing that I had passed that test and followed my intuition—flying through that storm at 200 mph in descent would have overwhelmed the engine.

Zen Moment

Having the courage to do a flight like this meant that I was not afraid to be bold, but I also knew I was taking a calculated risk and this clever maneuver could have some severe and unpredictable consequences. Still, I knew I was being guided.

Chapter 9

Waiting ... and Waiting

I held on for dear life as the camel I was riding lumbered side to side. We were navigating the immense pyramids of Cairo. I wore my Egyptian headscarf, which helped to block out some of the intense Egyptian heat and, happily, made for a good picture.

I'd be remiss not to mention that my camel was also a lover and happy to give a kiss. With prickly, dirty whiskers, bad breath and flies buzzing about, the kiss was an experience I will never forget. People found the pictures on Facebook entertaining and made all kinds of comments about my new hairy "girlfriend." What they didn't know was that my new "girlfriend" was appropriately named Charlie Brown, fitting him as a he!

Riding the camel was definitely an adventure and one that reminded me I was a world away from home. By this point in the trip, I was tired and showing some signs of wear and I was well aware that I had a long way to go. Eddie Gould had pushed hard for me to visit Egypt even though I had been before. He wanted to show me a good time in Egypt as it was his home turf.

Kissed by a camel in Egypt after a wild ride to see the Pyramids

Emotionally he provided me exactly the boost and reassurance I needed. We sat by the pool at the hotel drinking beer and talking about the British, the challenges I was having and the people before me that had made or attempted to make the trip. Eddie told me a story about a previous earth-rounder who had ripped his shorts climbing one of the pyramids. Fortunately, Eddie was able to get the shorts mended on the spot. He took pleasure in knowing he could handle any situation that arose including ripped shorts.

In the city we visited various museums as well as the central square where the second revolution riots that took the lives of many Egyptians had taken place. The people had risen up against President Mohamed Morsi and his Islamist government. The Muslim Brotherhood of Morsi had burned churches and killed foreigners; in the end, General Abdel Fattah el-Sisi stepped in and arrested Morsi and fought against the Muslim Brotherhood in street battles. After a year of military rule, Egypt had democratic elections, which Sisi, now a civilian, won.

Even so, the tension continued in the city making it feel like a powder keg that was ready to go off at any time. I could see anger and desperation on the faces of the people around me. As we entered and exited the area around the pyramids the day of the camel ride, random people tried to stop us by grabbing on to the car and yelling at us in an absolutely furious manner. We knew that they were scammers pretending to have authority at the various stops to grant us access and charge us fees. We ignored all of them and continued driving through. I was told later that one guy had held onto a car for an entire city block. Everywhere people were bouncing off a car like hail in a storm.

Due to an ISIS bombing I holed up in the hotel in Cairo for an entire day. It was chilling to know I was this close to the action, but given the undercurrent of anger I could feel, it didn't surprise me. Everywhere we went we saw stress on people's faces. The place was ready to erupt and I wanted out of this part of the world.

In spite of the tension around me, I found the hotel stay to be a welcome break from the stress of the trip and an opportunity to clean up a bit. I got a haircut that was one of the best ever, taking only fifteen minutes, complete with backrub. In addition, the barber held a piece of what looked like dental floss with his teeth and one hand to pull the random hairs from my eyebrows, ears and nose. This Egyptian version of tweezers was quite the spectacle. I was worried that one of his teeth would shoot out of his mouth as he yanked and maneuvered the thread around my face with great speed and accuracy.

On departure from Egypt the fueling happened in a reasonable period of time, but then I hit a wall with my clearance. Apparently the tower had to clear my route through some other international authority and they were in absolutely no hurry. I waited in the pilot seat in the sweltering 111-degree North African heat with the engine off, feeling the sweat drip from my forehead into my eyes. It was stinging my eyes, my shirt was soaking wet, and I hadn't even started my flight. Ahead of me was an eight-hour flight to India and already I felt fatigued.

This situation started making me angry. I lost track of the fact that I was on the most epic journey of a lifetime, one I was accomplishing by remaining focused only on the next leg. In fact, I honestly didn't have the brainpower to focus on more than that. Flying a high-performance plane in a foreign country, with questionable weather reporting, bad controllers, and little maintenance was about as much as I could handle.

Adding insult to injury, I was waiting with the plane's ground circuit, which was draining my battery minute by minute. I started to wonder if I would now have enough power for startup, and, since I was about a mile and a half from the nearest structure, if the battery died, how I would get the plane started. After fifteen minutes, I called to ask for my clearance. The response, from a female controller who seemed annoyed, was simply this: "N997MA—wait."

I waited another ten minutes, which gave me plenty of time to think about if I would ever again fly back to a place like Egypt. I had the sense that they didn't like me and they just didn't care. What had I done to make this happen? I had been friendly to the people, tipped generously, and spent many of my tourist dollars in their country. I had paid over six hundred dollars in handling fees and had posted on social media many times, reaching hundreds of thousands of people.

Once again I keyed the mic. "Cairo clearance delivery, November Niner Niner Seven Mike Alpha requesting clearance to Abu Dhabi." The response was as if swatting at a fly trying to get it to go away— "N997MA, clearance on request, wait!"

I responded with equal frustration, "November Niner Niner Seven Mike Alpha has 43 degrees Celsius temps in the cockpit and has been on hold for twenty-five minutes. Conditions are becoming critical."

No response … just the long hiss of the circuit. *Hsssssss.* By this time I was hot and pissed. I leaned out to talk to my handler, who had been sitting in his air-conditioned car with his smiling friend. I told them I felt like I was going to pass out from the heat. They replied that they could get a fan out to the plane in thirty to sixty minutes, but, of course, they would have to charge me for it, at which point they both started laughing.

Getting out of the cockpit and into the car with them was not an option as I could miss the call were it to come. After thirty-five minutes, I called and got the same female controller and told her I was minutes from declaring an emergency. This time I didn't even get a response. I asked to speak to the senior controller in the tower and another person came on to remind me that I was the captain of my aircraft. As such I was to do what was necessary for my own personal safety. At that point, the female controller came on the frequency to tell me, "Not my problem!"

I decided to start the plane and use its air conditioning, assuming the plane would start and taxi the mile to the run-up area. Of course I was now risking overheating the engine if I didn't get my clearance soon. Having traded fuel for comfort, I had no way to know how critically low on fuel I would be on the next leg of my trip. Once again I began to doubt myself. How was this fun? I was making life-and-death decisions almost every day! I felt that I had been lying to myself, thinking that this was a guaranteed good time. Nobody ever promised me that … it was simply a line of reasoning I had used to power me through the difficult and detailed planning portion of the trip.

Totally frustrated, I felt as if I was about to explode. Instead I leaned back in my seat, took a deep breath and asked myself, "What is the lesson here? What am I intended to learn so this will not upset me again? What is my part?" I was sure this was happening so I could heal it once and for all. And then I reminded myself that it was a blessing.

What came to me was I needed to learn patience and acceptance. I had little control over this situation. Clearance delivery was well aware of what I was going through and my responsibility now was determining how I would personally handle it. My anger had been distracting me from what lay ahead of me, an eight-and-a-half-hour flight where fuel would be tight and in a hostile part of the world. Getting angry was not going to help me. It would just cause me to make mistakes. I would be hurting my effort and myself by losing control.

If ever there was time to be a "Zen Pilot" it was now! I thought back to what it meant to be a "Zen Pilot":

Zen Pilots are those who Fly Thru Life answering a call to adventure while inspiring others. Zen Pilots have a quiet confidence that comes from knowing that they are guided and are on their unique path pursuing their passions.

Zen Pilots are brave enough to dream impossibly big and go after those dreams. They accomplish seemingly impossible tasks and goals with grace and ease.

Being a Zen Pilot is a way of being with yourself, others and the world that promotes open communication, gratitude, support and wonder.

A Zen Pilot applies insights gained from flying, travel, nature and silence to daily life, especially for the benefit of others.

That being said, I could reframe the situation by recognizing that clearance delivery was doing its best. I could use the time while I waited productively by tightening up the cockpit, familiarizing myself with the airport diagram to make sure I didn't burn extra fuel on my way out, or, as my handler suggested, getting outside the plane where it was cooler. There I could turn on my handheld radio and "cool down." Perhaps even "in joy" the day!

Many of us assume that our lessons stop when we embark on an epic journey, but the truth is our lessons accelerate because we now have the bandwidth to take on more. Our journey is one of learning that we must receive for ourselves—no one else can do it for us. We must carve our own path.

The final lesson here is to be thankful for the teachers who are brought into our lives to move us ahead in our evolution, even when they say it isn't their problem.

My lessons of patience would continue throughout the trip and I came to find that I had much more work to do.

Zen Moment

I felt as if I was going to explode. I took a deep breath and asked myself, "What is the lesson here? What am I intended to learn so this will not upset me again? What is my part?" What came to me was I needed to learn patience and acceptance. *Getting angry was not the solution.*

Zen Moment

Many of us assume that our lessons stop when we embark on an epic journey, but the truth is our lessons accelerate because we now have the bandwidth to take on more. Our journey is one of learning that we must receive for ourselves—no one else can do it for us. We must carve our own path.

Chapter 10

Healing Old Wounds

Finally I was flying from Egypt. I flew past Israel, then over Jordan, Saudi Arabia, Iran and Iraq, at which point I felt my stomach turn. It didn't really hit me why until I approached my destination, Qatar. I looked up at my Garmin G500 PFD and realized I had come back once again to the Persian Gulf region.

I remembered twenty-four years earlier, in 1991 during the first Gulf War that I served in the Navy as a young lieutenant. I spent many long days and nights on watch looking out at the oil-well fires that lit up the sky. The water, covered with oil, had sea snakes and jellyfish not to mention the occasional great white shark that would come out of the depths to gobble up the trash we threw overboard. It was unsettling to watch these sharks feed with enormously large mouths and protruding razor-sharp teeth. Knowing escape over the side if the ship took a hit was impossible kept the tension on board high.

It hit me that the reason for my coming back was that I needed to heal some old wounds, ones I had carried with me for a long time. Certainly my circumnavigation trip had many external purposes including fundraising for the Aircraft Owners and Pilots Association (AOPA) Scholarship fund called the Spirit of San Diego and, as well, for the Lindbergh Schweitzer Elementary School. But on a personal level, I was here for the purpose of letting go of these wounds.

And who would my teachers be? Everyone I had met so far who lived in North Africa and the Middle East, places like Morocco, Istanbul, Egypt, Qatar and Oman. It was time for me to resolve the judgments I had made years before about the Middle East during the Persian Gulf War. The stories and judgments I had made included biases about the people, their religion, the country and our reasons for fighting. Years had now passed, but I had spent little time processing it all. In my mind it was humanity at its worst, and I had some lingering guilt.

After some hard lessons in Oman I would come to realize that my antiquated way of seeing the Middle East had come from misinformation and fear. It was easy to see the world that way as a young naval officer during an armed conflict, but those views of the world no longer reflected where I was today. It was not based on love.

Don't get me wrong; there were some people that I felt were still carrying the same anger I had brought with me. But I met many more who had let it go, for example, the man who seated me in the hotel dining room in Istanbul. In the brief period of time I interacted with him I saw complete authenticity and compassion. Others included Abdulla, my taxi driver for four days in Egypt; the little girl at the pyramids; the pilot at the Qatar Flying Club; the man who genuinely smiled at me in the market; Faisal Ali Al Balushi from Oman Airports Management Company and all of the people who had sent me blessings online. This was all so healing that the experience of being there brought me to tears. If these people could forgive me, I could forgive them.

That time was part of our collective past, and now we had our present to embrace. We have all made mistakes and we are here to learn and evolve with the help of one another. None of us can change the past, and, in fact, the more we dwell on it the more we live in it. What a blessing to have these issues surface in us so that we can heal them. Keeping them tucked away inside only slows us down like rocks in a backpack.

Needless to say the air had cleared, the skies were blue, and the beaches were white once again. The energy had changed and I was seeing all this with a different set of eyes than in the past.

Zen Moment

We have all made mistakes and we are here to learn and evolve with the help of one another. None of us can change the past, and, in fact, the more we dwell on it the more we live in it. What a blessing to have these issues surface in us so that we can heal them. Keeping them tucked away inside only slows us down like rocks in a backpack.

Chapter 11

"Not My Problem"

My changed feelings about the Middle East would come from my absolute worst experience on the trip, one that took place in the oil-rich country of Oman. Eddie had warned me against stopping there during the planning phases of the trip. I explained that while in the Navy, as a surface warfare officer on the USS Leahy (CG-16), I wanted to be the officer that was selected every month to attend meetings ashore in Oman. My fellow officers had given the town rave reviews and I now wanted to check it out. I came to realize when I did visit that any place other than a US Navy warship during the Gulf War would have seemed like Shangri-La and worth bragging about when you made it back to the ship.

When I landed I was the only small aircraft on the tarmac. The others were all enormous commercial jets that were rolling in and out all day and night. It was like a herd of giant elephants surrounding a mouse trying to declare his rights and that size didn't matter!

The fueling companies at these large airports appeared to have enormous power and control of aviation because without fuel the planes aren't going anywhere. Without competition they could charge general aviation aircraft whatever they wanted and deliver it to them when and if they wanted. No amount of complaining, foot stomping, red-faced yelling, or prior notification seemed to help. The time I asked for a better price they just laughed and told me that the price is what it is.

I told them, "I am doing this flight to raise money so aspiring pilots can learn to fly, to make aviation cheaper for everyone, to bring people together."

"Not my problem," came the reply ... said with a grin. The big airlines had established contracts that covered thousands of gallons of fuel; obviously they were the priority, not the smaller general aviation aircraft that might land once a month. With so few general aviation aircraft in these countries it doesn't make sense for them to build smaller airports like the ones we have in the United States. Consequently, all aircraft, big and small, use the larger airports.

Aviation fuel was twenty dollars and sixty-six cents per gallon or $3,100 for the 150 gallons I needed. The fact that this country was oil rich made this pill even harder to swallow. "Mogas," which was high-octane car gas some lower performance planes used, was less than a dollar a gallon.

Unbeknownst to me, I had arrived four hours earlier than the handler expected due to some confusion about whether I was supposed to arrive at a particular local time or Coordinated Universal Time. (UTC is the standard by which the world regulates clocks and time on a twenty-four-hour basis.) When we requested handling services, our email response was that the handler was not able to provide *any* services during this busy time.

Once I landed and shut the plane down I was surprised that nobody came to greet me. It was extremely hot and I was soaking in perspiration as I sat for more than an hour under the wing waiting for some assistance. Clearly I was not a priority for anyone. I turned on the ground circuit and called the tower who redirected me to the ground frequency who finally referred me to the operations frequency.

I called operations three different times and each time someone said he would send a car. By my third request, after waiting for nearly an hour and draining my battery, I was as hot as the 110-degree weather. It was pretty clear to me that somewhere somebody was responding with a "Yah, yah, no problem" to my requests and did not intend to send anyone.

I began stopping cars that were passing my plane like a trail of ants frantically going to and from various parts of the airport to ask for assistance. The drivers would get on their radios and call some manager who never arrived. Finally, I stood in front of a police car that came to a sudden stop inches from me. Not surprisingly, he was agitated by my bold maneuver. I explained that I was concerned I was about to pass out and needed some help. He pointed me toward the fire station but didn't offer me transportation in his air-conditioned car. I could see this guy didn't like me. I then told him I was trying to get to the operations office. He stared at me for a few seconds and said a phrase I was becoming very familiar with, "Not my problem" and to get out of his way.

I said I would not get out of his way and "I was making it his problem."

He gave me an angry stare and I watched his left eye begin to twitch as he reached over to his gun and said, "Get out of my way, NOT MY PROBLEM."

I stepped out of his way and he drove off with a look on his face that I had not seen since the Persian Gulf War. I was beginning to accept that this was not a friendly place for me. The good luck, love and energy bubble in which I had been riding around the world was about to burst. My cherished Zen way of being was being tested and was about to take some hits.

One of the drivers that had gone by me earlier had motioned towards a nearby doorway. It was not labeled, but as it was only about two hundred feet away, I grabbed my bags and headed toward it. I was using my blue monogrammed Club Glove rolling luggage so in about sixty seconds I had zipped across the tarmac to this cement building with brown paint and no signs. I should have done it earlier, but I wanted to follow what I understood to be airport protocol.

As I swung the brown door open and could feel a gust of ice-cold air conditioning rush to hit me, I saw a startled look on everyone's face. I felt like yelling "Busted!" because for the last hour they had clearly seen me out on the tarmac and had done nothing. There were about ten people in the room, a couple of guys who were working and one more with his feet up on the desk. I later discovered that the one guy with his feet on the desk was the driver assigned to pick me up. I could hear the occasional crackle of the ground frequency circuit and, as I scanned the room looking for the source of the radio noise and found it, I knew instantly that I had found the person I had been talking to who had been promising me a car for the last hour.

I was soaked in sweat and could hardly contain my anger. The radio operator was frail, not more than five feet tall and about thirty years old with glasses and a beard. I was definitely not having a "Zen" moment when I realized that I wanted to toss him out into the heat and step on his glasses. He told me that he was upset with me for walking across the tarmac. Apparently it was not permitted even though it posed no risk to me.

We argued for a solid half hour about the services I had not been provided including fuel, waiting in the heat as well as whether or not I was in fact early. At times we both did the angry arm-waving dance. He had a copy of the email and had underlined the part with the timeframe that had some unclear language. I could see where the misunderstanding came from, but it had become clear that the conversation was going nowhere and that they were not going to fuel my plane during this busy time. The men asked me to move my plane, which was taking up a spot for one of the larger planes, to a new location on the other side of the airport, a couple miles away. I knew if I moved my plane it would never get fueled and I would be stuck even farther away. The only bargaining power I had was to keep the plane right where it was and disrupt their operations to the point they would have to deal with me. This squeaky wheel was going to get the Middle Eastern oil.

I told them that my big turbo-charged engine did worse than I did in this heat and it would never start until it was fueled. This was a big problem for them with huge commercial 777 planes coming and going every few minutes. Still they refused to fuel my plane anytime soon. I threw up my hands and told the handlers I was going to my hotel. The short guy with glasses gave me the same answer he had before, which was that he had called for transportation. By being difficult I hoped they would want to get me out of there sooner so they could go back to a leisurely putting their feet on the table pace. I told them I would wait another thirty minutes and then I was going to walk to the terminal, which was about double the distance I had just walked. That, they said, was not permitted and they would call the police.

During this thirty-minute countdown, I worked on my cell phone and managed to snap a picture of one of them with his feet on the table. I figured it would make for an interesting story at some future point. At five minutes, I gave them a warning, then picked up my bags and walked to the terminal.

After converting my cash at the currency exchange, I got into the passport line. I had progressed to second in line when a police officer, his hand on his gun, instructed me to step out of the line and follow him. He looked nervous but had a "don't make me do it" look on his face and would not take no for an answer. I began to rethink the stink I made in the operations office. Having someone pull me out of line with his hand on his gun was enough to cause a huge scene and I was still steaming from the way I had been treated over the last couple hours. Had the guy not had a gun I would have ignored him, but he did have one and I did what he said. The policeman ushered me into a room where a number of officials were slowly gathering. What I didn't realize was they were setting up for a trial and I would be representing myself!

Approximately eleven people gathered over the next thirty minutes—three police officers in uniform, the five-foot guy with glasses and a beard, four guys in white robes and two administrators in suits. The guys in the white robes seemed to be the most senior and were asking questions and recording answers in Arabic. One of them had been educated in the US and was doing some translating.

The airport operations office in Muscat, Oman. Workers sit talking in air conditioned comfort watching for over an hour as I endure the 114 F temperatures on the black tarmac. The driver of the car that was intended to pick me up sits with his feet on the table relaxing.

In response to their questions, I told my story in great detail. At the thirty-minute mark, I stopped and said, "There are eleven of you and just one of me. Surely you have something better to do than hassle me instead of providing the services I have contracted." They replied that they had procedures they needed to follow and why had I breached them? I pulled out my phone and found the picture of all of them sitting on their rears with their feet up and explained that this was what they were doing as I waited an hour for a four hundred-foot ride to the terminal. Apparently, it was forbidden to take a picture of their operations center.

The next few minutes involved lots of arm waving and people shouting and shaking their heads. While my picture made them look bad, it once again came back to yet another reason to arrest me. My list of discrepancies was growing as were my visions of being assigned to a work camp in the desert breaking rocks with a sledgehammer for the next thirty years. I was finally able to get them to calm down when I agreed to delete the picture. (My iPhone of course stored a backup copy, which I have included.) They continued to ask me to move my plane; now after four hours the engine was certainly cool.

I pointed out that in the four hours since I had landed the airport was no longer busy and they could fuel me without my moving the plane. I was now using their timeline email against them and they decided to send the English-speaking translator to the office to try to expedite the fueling. I stressed to them that if they would simply honor their promise for services we could all go about our business. I could go to my hotel and they could continue with observations of their religious holiday of Ramadan. As a month-long event, Ramadan had been causing me delays and problems all the way through North Africa and the Middle East.

Still no action. In fact, they once again asked me to move my plane. This time I responded with another reason that I could not comply. The fuel was so low in the tanks that if I attempted to start the engine, it would pull dirt up from the bottom of the tanks and would certainly clog the injectors and then the plane would never be moved. Understand that the story I was telling was not true, but I made a convincing argument.

The white-robed English speaker came over to me to say he had worked a deal with the fuel guys and that they would take care of me later that day. I said since they had now breached *two* promises to fuel me I would be foolish to trust them a third time. Furthermore, why would they park me where they could not fuel my plane? They ignored my questions as they were the ones asking me their questions.

I went on to tell about the police officer who put his hand on his gun and told me to get out of the way. They asked for his name and I replied that I didn't know as I was focused on his gun, not his name tag. One of the white robes was busy writing from right to left in Arabic to record the conversation. I asked them if they thought I would make up a story like this, that I was enjoying being interrogated at the airport when I could be at my hotel room resting up or sightseeing.

I sat back in my seat wondering how this was all going to end. At eleven against one, it was not looking good for me. For an instant, I felt my eyes start to tear up. I realized if they saw me getting emotional I would lose the respect of everyone in the room. I turned my head away to regain my composure, fearful that I might be earning my way into a prison cell for several days. The stress was starting to get to me and I was reaching my limit, tired from the flight and the time in the intense sun. But I kept up my act of being the upset American who was incensed that I would be treated in this way in a foreign country. After all, I was on a mission of goodwill! I had a flashback to my earlier raging that got me nowhere and knew I had to get this ploy under control. It was tough to know what to do as I was unaware of their customs and had no idea what would get me into more serious trouble.

The questioning continued for almost an hour; they would on occasion circle back and ask me the same questions almost as if to check for consistency in my story. Any American who watches daytime crime TV knows this technique and I was not about to let a room full of these men outsmart me!

Eventually some more senior people entered the room. I could see they were the people that were more benevolent and had the authority to make this go away. Their faces were friendly as they greeted everyone in the room. I was sure these weren't people who were tasked with simply following the rules.

I explained to them that I chose my health and safety over their rules. And that had I complied, by now I would have been horizontal on their tarmac and they would have bigger issues to deal with … this caused several of them to pause and reflect.

They attempted to get me to sign a document that they had written up in Arabic. Waving my hand and shaking my head, I said I would *never* sign that document. Finally the senior guy in the room decided that this circus had gone on long enough as he told me their country was one of "hospitality." He believed that I would be fueled in a few hours and that I could wait in the police office until it was time for that. I was led to the airport police office where the officers were cordial to me and just trying to do their jobs. I explained to them several times that I wanted to leave; they continued to tell me to wait a little longer. Fed up and exhausted I watched the clock for the next two hours.

Still nothing!

That was it—I had reached my limit. I decided to try once again what hadn't worked with the five-foot guy with glasses and a beard a few hours earlier. Yes, I would be doubling down and again bluffing, but I would allow this to escalate to the next level. In a burst of false confidence and American bravado, I stood up and declared that I was a US citizen being held against my will! Pounding my fist on the table I told them I wanted my passport and if they held me a minute longer I wanted to contact my embassy! I tried to get them to say I was being "held," in a performance so convincing I was starting to believe it myself.

Finally I had found words that seemed to scare them more than anything that had transpired. I had hit a nerve and I knew it. In their police office at the airport I was in control for the first time. The officers went immediately outside and had a frantic conversation. I could see arms waving as the men leaned in toward one another, blaming the other I'm sure for the situation I had created. Voices were rising and although I couldn't understand their

Arabic, it was obvious they were upset. All of a sudden their rules were not that important anymore. After all, an international incident was possibly unfolding and it would take them days to unwind this one if it went any further. At long last I was feeling satisfied—I had finally beaten these guys.

A short time later the administrator in a green suit walked me through the airport, telling me how he had always worked on my behalf. I made it outside the airport and got into a taxi with the feeling that I had just been given a get-out-of-jail free card. I vowed right then never to lose my cool again in a Middle Eastern country. Yes, I was free, but I had paid the price in grey hair, stress, time and frustration. It was hardly a victory and I suspect with a bit more patience I could have avoided the entire circus.

By the next day in Oman a wonderful shift had occurred. I had a few good meals, a good night's sleep and a chance to reflect. I went to the airport control center where I met the senior guy and watched him direct many others with absolute confidence. He had several young good-looking assistants that reminded me of the junior officers on my ship during the Gulf War. Everybody was highly trained and things were happening very precisely.

I told the lead guy that he was the "Great Oz," how he was the one man getting more done than anybody at the airport—that he knew more than anybody there. I tried to explain what it meant to be the "Great Oz," though I'm not sure he understood. In any case, he and I became friends as I did as well with his assistants.

One by one they talked to me. One shared pictures of the fish he had caught free diving. He was looking forward to his next trip and learning to hold his breath even longer. It hit me that these guys were me at that age. They reminded me very much of my time in the military, trying to do the best job they could, working their way up the chain of command, following orders and making a better life for themselves. They weren't the devil as I had viewed them on the first day.

I had been promised fueling on the day I arrived at 10:30 a.m., noon, 3:00 p.m., 5:00 p.m. The following day I was promised 8:00 a.m. and finally at 10:00 a.m. My bill came to $3,100 for 150 gallons of Avgas. I vowed never to complain again about the cost of fuel or the fifteen-to-thirty minute wait I sometimes experience in the United States. At this point, I realized that Avgas burners were a thing of the past and not the way to do a trip around the world. Avgas—or Aviation Gas—was becoming harder and harder to find outside the United States. Its availability dictated in part my route around the world. Jet A or Diesel was far more common and much cheaper. At some point it makes sense to convert all aviation engines to Jet A burners. From this point forward, I decided that I must find a solution for future trips.

Zen Moment

I felt like I had just been given a get-out-of-jail free card. I vowed never to lose my cool again in a Middle Eastern country. I was free, but I had paid the price in grey hair, stress, time and frustration. It was hardly a victory and I'm sure I could have avoided the entire circus if I had been a little more patient.

Chapter 12

A Critical Mistake

On my flight from Nagpur, India to Subang, Malaysia I was almost midway to my destination, when I made a major mistake that put the flight and my life in danger. I was about nine hundred miles out to sea and had burned off the fuel in my tip tanks as well as the ninety gallons I was carrying in my main ferry tank. I shifted to one of my wing "main" tanks.

A few minutes later I looked at the fuel valve and saw that the fuel gauge read twenty gallons of fuel. I had just *lost* forty gallons of fuel over the Pacific and had no idea where it went. Fred Sorenson had told me that if I misaligned my fuel valves, I ran the risk of pumping the fuel out of the plane through the fuel vents located at the bottom of each wing tip. This could happen quickly as the fuel pumps were capable of moving large amounts of fuel. I had just made a critical mistake. I had forgotten to close the valve on the ferry tank!

Robert DeLaurentis, Zen Pilot somewhere over India, bored, scared, hungry, tired and unshaven, sitting in front of a ferry tank loaded with 140 gallons of high octane aviation fuel. On top of the ferry tank was a high frequency radio (an ignition source), separated by a thin ¼ inch piece of plywood. The potential for explosion was enormous.

The thought flashed through my mind of natural selection where dumb pilots kill themselves off by taking ridiculous risks and making mistakes. I was out over the Bay of Bengal judging myself an "idiot" as my fear and panic begin to fully express themselves. I could feel my stomach tighten up and move instantly to my throat as I took a series of short panic breaths and thought about how screwed I was.

My fortunes improved after a careful review of my Pilot's Operating Handbook (POH). I slowed my plane to the speed of a much slower and less capable Cessna 182. My fuel burn dropped from twenty-two gallons an hour to just fourteen. This would extend my range as well as my flight time. I began calculating my increased range with the slower fuel burn and riding the currents of the earth. It was like a magic carpet ride but in *slow* motion. I wasn't in a hurry, but I wondered what the people that were following the trip would begin to think when I didn't land in eight hours as expected. They would be waiting two-and-one-half additional hours and most likely wondering what happened to me.

The Garmin G500 primary flight display shows of the "Spirit of San Diego" arriving in the Persian Gulf region unprepared for what awaited her.

I got a frantic text from Eddie Gould. He was sweating bullets rapid fire! Like a mother bird preparing her chicks for flight, he was 100 percent there with me on every flight. Eddie would stay up to make sure I landed safely no matter where I was in the world.

I landed just over three hours late in the darkness of Malaysia, weary from a ten-and-one-half hour flight. The airport was largely deserted by this time, but a member of the Experimental Aircraft Association (EAA) Malaysia met me. He was friendly and helped get me fueled for the next leg, took me to get some local currency, a bite to eat and then to my hotel. I was successful in completing the challenge the Universe had sent my way. I was now being given an opportunity to rest for what would be the biggest challenge of the trip.

I realized that life happens in "God-time"— not on our schedule. Events unfold in the exact order they need to so we can learn our lessons. Certain things must happen first before the desired outcome can manifest. This God-time can take an instant, hours or days. We are not in control.

Zen Moment

I realized that life happens in "God-time"—not on our schedule. Events unfold in the exact order they need to so we can learn our lessons. Certain things must happen first before the desired outcome can manifest. This God-time can take an instant, hours or days. We are not in control.

Chapter 13

Tested

My day started out like many others on my trip. After jumping through a bunch of customs and immigration hoops, paying inflated landing, airport and other fees to people I would never get to know or see again, I was departing at about 10 a.m. from Subang International Airport in Kuala Lumpur.

This was close to the two-thirds mark of my trip and I was happy to be past the Middle East and Northern Africa. I looked forward to Australia and some remote Pacific islands where I would just lie on a beach, drink piña coladas and gather all the legs of the trip together in my mind. Life would be slowing down and I looked forward to it. I would use this quiet time to accelerate my learning beyond the point I thought was possible to even absorb.

The Universe had other intentions.

The local media had interviewed me and I would be on TV the next day and in the newspaper the following day. I was getting good with these interviews and had just sung praises to everyone that had helped me including the shop that was about to put me into the most harrowing and terrifying ten-minute struggle of my life. Lots of smiling faces everywhere, lots of thank yous and I felt like I had a family in Malaysia. Aren't you always safe with family?

I went through my preflight checklist as I had many times before. Magnetos were hot and I pressed the starter. The engine started, lights on the dash came to life, I could hear the crackle of the radio and I was again reminded how fortunate I was to be seated firmly in one extremely high performance twin-turbocharged single-engine piston aircraft.

As I taxied away from the hanger with all the waving supporters I was also waving a flag I had been given by a member of EAA Malaysia who had supported me during my stay. It was a kind gesture and I was feeling blessed. I ran up the aircraft and taxied away, as always. The performance was strong. I was happy knowing that my plane had the much-needed oil change as well as the spark plugs cleaned. I was expecting stronger performance on takeoff than I had been experiencing. I taxied to Runway 15 and looked out over the 12,402 feet ahead of me thinking to myself, "Piece of cake."

By this time I was comfortable flying 10 percent over max gross and I had a plane that was working well. I was well rested and ready for my next adventure. The tower cleared me: "November Niner Niner Seven Mike Alpha, cleared for IFR release Runway 15." I pushed the throttle and mixture forward and listened to the engine increase in rpms. The engine was developing good horsepower and the plane seemed to pull hard down the runway, rotate and climb out strongly. I was doing the published instrument departure procedure and noting to myself how my piloting skills had improved on this trip.

Departure control called for a climbing right turn at three thousand feet and then I was directed in the opposite direction of my intended "on course" heading. I had a few minutes to snap some pictures of the coast as I passed eight thousand feet. I was headed to Indonesia, the country where I had spent two years growing up. I was excited to see the country again and to visit my old house where I had many adventures as a young boy. I was constantly getting myself into trouble whether it was egging the neighbor's house, throwing ropes up on the power lines and getting them to arc when they touched, grabbing fish out of our fish ponds with my bare hands, teasing our pet monkey "Benny" or jumping through a glass window with a cape pretending to be Superman. I escaped the window incident with having only to pay for the replacement glass out of my allowance. I think my parents thought that the big red cherry on my forehead was punishment enough. I don't know what conclusions can be drawn from my childhood except that the punishment didn't stop me from the adventures and that I am still a risk taker.

Engine out over water

I had been flying for about twenty minutes when something flickered out of the right side of my eye: the yellow oil pressure warning light.

About a second later the light went solid and the propeller instantly oversped. My stomach shot to my throat and my body violently slammed against my seatbelt straps. The plane slowed as if somebody had hit the emergency brakes hard.

The oil that fed the propeller hub had been lost and the propeller instantly went flat. Now instead of providing thrust, it became a giant seven-foot rotating brake.

I was rocketing to the sea sitting in an aircraft loaded six hundred pounds beyond its maximum landing weight limit with high-octane aviation fuel just a foot behind me and to the right. It was as if somebody had just started the clock, which was counting how long I had to live. I was literally falling to the ground without power and I couldn't stop it. All I could do was negotiate where the impact would happen.

My two worst fears as a pilot were occurring at the exact same moment in time: ENGINE OUT! SINGLE ENGINE PLANE OVER THE WATER!

My mind was racing. I would potentially have to ditch in the ocean and I knew my chances for survival were not good with most people being knocked out on impact and only one minute until the plane submerges. I was experiencing an in-flight emergency! This was what sheer and total panic and terror felt like. Sweat was dripping down my back and the smell of perspiration and fear was everywhere. I felt like I was in a game I didn't want to play.

I looked over to the right side of the cockpit and saw nobody. I was totally alone. I don't think I was ever so alone in my life. At that moment I realized that I wasn't alone, fear was with me the entire time, my constant companion. When I passed on to my next life I wanted to be surrounded by loved ones, in a bed having a tender loving moment, not being taken in this violent abortion of reality.

A random thought popped into my mind, which had never seemed to leave me since I had heard it years before in Narsarsuaq, Greenland. A pilot I met there said to me, "No matter how bad it gets, never give up."

I remembered the advice, "Action is the antidote to fear" (from Michael McCafferty's *The Spirit of Adventure*), so I quickly reached up to pull the rpm lever back, but it was jammed. It didn't move an inch. Of course, it couldn't work without the lifeblood that the oil provided. Silly for me to think that would fix anything. I knew better, but I had to try.

I could see flashing lights and hear sirens going off in the cockpit: *Neeer Eeer Neeer Eeer!* God damn that engine, why won't it slow down I thought? Where did the eleven quarts—almost three gallons of oil—go? Would the cockpit be filling with smoke? Was the oil about to spray on the windshield? Should I be expecting an engine fire in flight? I was terrified to see what was coming next. I didn't even want to think that. I didn't want to be manifesting any of these things!

I knew nobody could save me except me. I felt that this was happening for somebody's entertainment to see how I would perform, that the gods were testing me. Damn God and damn the fucking Universe, I thought. Once the game had been started it could not be stopped. Why me? Why now? And I didn't want to be playing any game with my life. I didn't want to go this way.

I began to doubt my abilities as a pilot, that I was a great or even good pilot. Could it be that the flight to twenty countries prior to this trip hadn't made me a better pilot? I had just been lucky. That was the story running in my head. I felt awkward in the cockpit, something I hadn't felt since my beginning flight training five years before. The life-and-death game of flying had an efficient way of weeding out pilots with flying flaws or gaps in their training. At least I was alive at this moment in time and I was thankful for that. I needed to focus on what was happening now. Fate was dealing me an ugly hand.

I had heard at various times during my training that by the time the low oil pressure light comes on the engine is shot. Most pilots will never experience an engine out in flight. Commercial pilots who fly thousands of hours in large aircraft will likely lose only one of their two to four engines in their entire careers. But me, with just 1,200 hours? Was fate serving me up something that I was destined to experience? I had a fleeting hope that perhaps this nightmare would just stop, the light would go off. That sometimes happens in planes. Contacts are dirty, old or stop working once—and then randomly come back to life. Nobody can explain it and so we pass it off to the gremlins that live inside. But the light was on solid now and I couldn't believe my eyes. In a strange way, I knew that at some point on my flight I would be dealing with a major event, that I would be tested. In my spiritual psychology studies I had learned the technique of blocking thoughts by yelling the words, "Cancel, cancel!" But all the cancels in the world were not changing my reality.

Little did I know, the eleven quarts of oil were being dumped on the hot exhaust of the right front cylinder. The temperature on the exhaust was in excess of 1,500 degrees Fahrenheit. What act of God was preventing that oil from catching on fire?

Altitude is life and I had about five to ten minutes of reserve time before the plane would impact the ground. There were more than one hundred decisions to make in those minutes that would seal my fate. Facing me were four possible outcomes. Destruction of the plane and I could die, destruction of the plane and I would be injured, destruction of the plane and I walk away or I could put this plane heavily laden with fuel down and walk away unhurt.

The fact that I was over water and a turn to the left would put me over the jungle greatly decreased my chances for survival. Airports in this country were few and far between and the likelihood of getting to one was virtually impossible.

I was involved in a cosmic negotiation to walk away with all my limbs and a working plane, but I knew as with any negotiation you rarely get everything you are asking for. My request of the Universe seemed unrealistic and almost selfish. I started to think about what I was willing to give up in order to walk away alive.

My first thought was, *Holy shit, it was happening and I knew it would.* It was always just a matter of when. The plane had been working perfectly. In fact, it had been working as well as it ever had on the climb out. Gauges were where they needed to be and I seemed to have a surplus of power. After all they had just cleaned the spark plugs. My mind drifted again and I started thinking about how much I loved the *Spirit of San Diego*, the plane that was now going to test my skills as a pilot and a person on this planet.

When I first contacted the air traffic control tower it was if they couldn't hear what I had said. I repeated my first call. "November Niner Niner Seven Mike Alpha has no oil pressure—request vector nearest airport!" When I finally got a vector from the ATC it was behind me at the airport I had just left called Subang. I knew with the altitude I had remaining I could not glide back to Subang. I could bleed off in a glide somewhere between twelve thousand to fourteen thousand feet of altitude. That would get me one-and-a-half to two nautical miles for every thousand feet but that calculation didn't include a flat prop that created an enormous amount of drag. This was going to be damn close!

I would later find out that apparently commercial traffic delays were more important than my life. The air traffic controller did not want to tie up a busy airport like Kuala Lumpur International 2 with a small six-seater single-engine aircraft wreckage that was hemorrhaging hot black engine oil at a fantastic rate and could contaminate and close down their runway. However, even in my moment of panic I could determine Subang was not the closest airport. I found the nearest airport by hitting the "direct to" button on my Garmin GTN 750 touch screen GPS and then "nearest airport" button. The display instantly showed Kuala Lumpur International 2 and read 19.6 nautical miles. It was a big international airport jammed with large commercial planes. I was about to be a small plane among giants and the most important person in that entire airport.

I hit the direct-to button; the autopilot did not respond. After a few more attempts I abandoned the autopilot. I was hand flying. I turned the nose towards the airport and clicked the microphone button, "Negative, November Niner Niner Seven Mike Alpha needs direct Kuala Lumpur International". I thought to myself I just need confirmation that I'm headed in the right direction. Didn't they know I was having an in-flight emergency?

I could feel a sense of panic and fear setting in that I knew would be of no use to me in that situation … damn that autopilot, I thought. I was frantically hitting buttons and I didn't know if the lights and sirens were distracting me so that I was simply not able to push the correct buttons in the proper sequence. I had all this technology and it was failing me. I decided to use my knees to steer the plane along the magenta GPS line and was manually adjusting the descent rate using the trim. Optimum glide rate was 90 knots. Damn the repair shop that just changed the oil! I'm reading zero pounds oil pressure that will cook my turbochargers that are spinning at 90,000 rpm each. The turbos were either going to seize, blow up, catch on fire or some combination of those things. I figured I had just a minute or two more until something catastrophic happened.

Still in shock, I knew I had selected the closest airport on my GPS, but I wanted to confirm I had the correct information. Was there a smaller airport that my GPS hadn't picked up because I had set parameters for larger airports? The air traffic control tower came back with a vector that was now 10 degrees off my heading to Kuala Lumpur International 2. The controller asked, "N997MA are you declaring an in-flight emergency?"

I responded, "Affirmative!!!"

The air traffic controllers would place six commercial airliners in holds from their approaches into Kuala Lumpur International 2 from the point that I declared an in-flight emergency. The law of gross tonnage no longer applied and no matter how big the planes were that now circled Kuala Lumpur, I was the most important person and plane within one hundred miles and I was coming in by the grace of God.

My thinking at that point was to be grateful. I was alone, nobody to see me afraid or make a mistake. "I can die with some dignity except for the panicked sound of my voice that is being blasted all over the airways."

Kuala Lumpur approach came back with a vector that put me well behind the airport as if I was being set up on an instrument approach for Runway 15. For a third time, I said, "Negative direct Kuala Lumpur." I was not going to follow their instructions that would put me either in the water, jungle or somewhere short of the airport. I would choose the option that put me closest to the most people that could help me—right down the center of their longest and closest runway. I knew that they were scrambling the airport emergency workers, fire trucks and anybody with medical training. This was the real deal.

I adjusted my course to follow the magenta line on my GPS display that took me to Kuala Lumpur International 2 for my next challenge which was landing over gross with six hundred pounds of extra fuel. How funny I thought that the line was magenta. Magenta represents love in the spiritual world. This line that I frantically tried to follow was going to bring me to a place of love?

Enough with that. I was being tested and it was time for me to get on with my test. I throttled back to see if that would stop the over speeding propeller. No sense in running the engine hard with no oil. I would reduce the torque on the engine and try to save it for when I needed it if at all. Just like our hearts need blood to pump to our vital organs, a Lycoming IO-540 needs oil and large amounts to lubricate and cool this 350-hp twin turbocharged fire-breathing dragon!

No change! Damn!

Before the flight I had felt compelled to put three quarts of oil behind the pilot seat that I could reach back and grab. My plane in ferry configuration could pump oil from the pressurized cabin into the engine in flight. I was still flying the plane with my knees. This was something I had never done before. I thought I was again being betrayed by technology and forced back into the time of Lindbergh when autopilots didn't exist.

As I turned my attention to the task at hand, which was getting more lifeblood to the engine, I frantically reached behind my seat trying to feel for the three quarts of oil I had placed there. Not being very flexible I stretched as I rotated with my seat belts trying to hold me firmly in place. Finally my hand found a quart of AeroShell 15W-50 oil and I brought it forward and frantically screwed the black top off. I needed to find a secure place to set the bottle so that it would not fall over and waste the golden fluid that was possibly the key to my survival. I wedged the bottle between the copilot seat and the carpet runner that ran between the seats.

Next, I looked for the clear plastic feeder hose to put into the oil. It had a black plastic tip that ensured it didn't collapse when I put the tube into the oil and turned the pump on. All of this was in a big black plastic bag so it wouldn't get oil all over the cockpit. I dug through this plastic bag looking for the assembly when, a valuable couple seconds later, I found the feeder line and inserted it into the oil, opened the red valve to the engine supply line and was finally ready to turn on the pump.

Alternating looking up to make sure I was still on my glide slope and the magenta line to not lose critical altitude gliding into Kuala Lumpur International 2, I found the small black toggle switch on the supplemental oil pump with the on/off marking. It certainly was not on and I prayed that it had not been on the entire time and burnt out from having no oil going to it. I would have never been able to hear if it had mistakenly gotten turned on with all that cockpit noise.

I flipped the oily switch and I heard it go *wirrrrrrrrrrlllll*. Almost immediately I could see the oil start to flow from the quart bottle through the winding clear hose to the red value leading to the engine. The pump whirled for the longest thirty seconds of my life and then it started to cavitate and spin even faster. I picked up the quart bottle and tilted it on its side to ensure every last drop of this life-giving fluid made it to the engine. The oil flowed for a split second more then I heard the wirrrrrrrrrrlllll again. The pump had resumed cavitating and I shut it down to keep it from burning out. I was still in a panic when I looked up and saw the oil pressure gauge still read a great big *zero!*

I reached behind me and started the process all over with the next can of oil. The gauge didn't move from zero. As I turned for the final quart Kuala Lumpur approach came on and offered another bad vector that was about 10 degrees off. I ignored him. I was busy unscrewing the bottle top, wedging it upright, inserting the feeder tube, and again, *wirrrrrrrrrrrrrrlll.* I looked up and the oil pressure gageread "40 psi!!" It was not the 65 psi I needed, but it was better than nothing! I might need a bit more power out of that engine. It could be the difference between life and death.

Checking my glide slope and course I saw I had been doing a relatively good job of staying on course at the proper decent rate. Glide speed was 94 knots, not bad. At least I was no longer over the water, but my situation might now be worse since I was over the jungle with hundred foot trees densely packed. Hitting one was the equivalent of hitting a wall head on. I was back to calculating in my head my glide distance at seven miles and this elevation. Now I was six miles out and alternating from thinking I was doing a good job to being panicked and not doing very well. I looked up and could just see haze and not the patterns that indicated an airport. I made a slight correction to the right with my knees. Back on the magenta love line!

I had always been taught to prioritize in this order: Aviate, navigate and then communicate. Now I was ready to turn my attention back to the air traffic controller. He had been distracting me with erroneous vectors and constant calls, but I made a decision to talk to him one last time and then I was done. He came back with a vector five degrees off. Did he really want me to set me up for an approach I thought? My voice cracked back with the intensity of lightning. "Negative! November Niner, Niner Seven Mile Alpha is direct Kuala Lumpur! I'm coming in, clear all aircraft . . . final communication!!"

Nothing is more terrifying to other pilots that to hear another aircraft in distress. It hits way too close to home. Deep down we know the risks we are taking. It may seem like fun and games, but it is the real thing. Every time we step into our flying machines we are taking our lives into our own hands and it's a calculated risk. Lindbergh knew it, Earhart knew it, and every pilot knows it.

Finally the airport appeared out of the haze. The runway was long, over twelve thousand feet!

And it was my safe harbor. Although it was still questionable if I would make it, I now felt I had a fighting chance. The issue was that I was over gross with an extra ninety gallons of high octane aviation fuel in my ferry tank just inches away from me plus my full mains and tip tanks. I was too heavy to land. I could take off over gross, but landing that heavy I was told would collapse the gear and then I would be sliding on the belly of the plane creating sparks and heat with wings dragging that were full of fuel.

God, could I get it to the runway and then have to deal with a fire? Would my ferry tank that was strapped down inside the cabin hold or would it come shooting forward at 80 knots if I hit hard? Should I put on my goggles to prevent the fuel from burning my eyes?

This would have to be the smoothest landing of my life. My touchdown speed needed to be precisely 80 knots (92 mph).

The sound in the cockpit was deafening with the different horns that were going off and the chatter on the radio. Most of the air traffic had been shifted to another frequency. I could make out the low manifold pressure horn since I had throttled back to save the engine for when I needed it. The terrain warning voice was saying, "Terrain pull up, pull up!" And behind that I could hear a higher-pitched sound. Lights flashing, horns blaring! This was a first-rate shit storm and nobody could do anything about it besides me. *Why me, why now? This is what panic feels like!* To be this close to death and know it for five minutes beforehand was unbearable. During all of this I was so focused on the plane, so very much in the moment. How could this wonder of modern technology with all its goodies let me down? Betray me?

Looking at the airport in the distance, I said, "Thank you God!" I even thought to pull out my cell phone and record some of my engine readings for the mechanic to review. This information would be critical and could tell them if the engine could be saved. The airport was coming clearly into view, a big one that was set up for smaller commercial traffic like 737s. I could see the runway markers and number on this immense runway ahead of me. All I would be required to do was make an 80-degree turn to the right, and do my standard "GUMPS" landing checklist. Aviation had many acronyms. "GUMPS" stood for Gas (check that the fuel pump is on, you have selected fullest tank), Undercarriage (landing gear down and you have three lights indicating green confirming their position), Mixture (fuel lever is forward set for takeoff setting in case you have to go around), Prop (forward set for high rpm needed for takeoff), and Seatbelts (as tight as you can get your lap belt).

I was about to do what I had done hundreds of times before, but this time was the only time that I would land the plane over the max gross weight. I looked back at this enormous fuel tank about a foot behind me and to the right. I thought a gallon of high-octane aviation gas was enough to cook me, but I was carrying ninety. This was a huge amount of stress for anyone to live through. I was experiencing many new things I certainly did not want to add crash landing to my resume.

I had a vision of this fuel tank bursting and splashing aviation fuel all over the hot avionics. It was okay to take off heavy since you were just rolling with the extra weight. But I was now required to set the plane down on the landing gear, which was the weakest part of the aircraft. Nobody had approved this kind of punishment for the plane. Not the FAA, not Piper, not my mechanic. Nobody in his or her right mind would tell you do to this.

My request was coming directly from the Universe and "No" was not an option.

Zen Moment

I was involved in a cosmic negotiation and would ask for the very best outcome, but I knew as with any negotiation you rarely get everything you are asking for. My request of the Universe seemed unrealistic and almost selfish. Who was I to get it all in this negotiation? I started to think about what I was willing to give up in order to walk away alive.

Starting at KMYF (San Diego) flying to 23 countries, five continents and crossing more than 12 oceans and seas.

Gibraltar Airport, managed by the British Military, sits on the peninsula of Gibraltar, a British overseas territory that borders Spain. Africa is in the distance.

Robert proudly standing next to "The Spirit of San Diego" in front of
the Rock of Gibraltar

Staying safe and healthy with the help of sponsors Lightspeed Aviation, Garden of Life, and Scheyden Precision Eyewear.

Lindbergh Schweitzer Elementary Presentation at Landmark Aviation

Press Conference at Landmark Aviation upon my safe return to
San Diego

Wearing official Malaysian airport apparel

Malaysia Officials after Emergency Landing

Glass instrument panel on the "Spirit of San Diego"

Chapter 14

Landing Heavy

I had never trained to land an aircraft heavy and nowhere would there be anything in writing probably because people would assume that meant there was a way to do it, and that's a very bad idea. It's like loading a car up with massive cement blocks and then driving over a wooden bridge that was certified to the exact weight of the car *empty*, not with the extra six hundred pounds. The thousand-foot gorge below would be your punishment if the bridge collapsed. Add to all of this, the sweat is running down your back, the smell of fear surrounds you as your body lets out a unique and terrible odor and you're trembling as you consider what is about to happen. Now hyper alert you know your entire life is dependent on the moment that is about to unfold.

If ever there was a moment that would define me it was seconds away.

I was moving through the air in a 4,900-pound flying bomb and it was my job to get it back on the ground without it blowing it and me to pieces in a fiery cloud of billowing black flames and noxious burning aluminum.

I hated the Universe in this moment and wondered if I had done something to deserve this. Little did I know I was in the hands of God about to be taught one of my valuable lessons of my life. I looked out at each side of the forty-three-foot wingspan and thought to myself, "I'm landing on angel wings". Everything seemed to turn into slow motion. For a second, I was weightless and floating. Everybody who had followed me was holding me up. My mother who had passed years before, my family and friends, my sponsors and all the people whose names I didn't even know that were watching. I was on the wings of love.

As I felt the landing gear mains gently touch down followed a couple seconds later by the ever-so-fragile nose wheel, I knew that my soul had just reconnected with the earth. I was safe. The plane was intact, the landing gear had held, the ferry tank had not exploded, I had no physical injuries. I had won the cosmic lottery. My plane and I had survived. I was in shock, unable to comprehend all that had just happened. I was gulping deep breaths, perspiring and thinking this is what it feels like to be alive. I thanked God for each second he was giving me. As I rolled off the runway, I watched the oil pressure needle flicker between zero and 20 psi.

I shut the idling engine down. Radio off, cooling fan off, magnetos off, alternators off. The engine stopped and I could hear the gyros start to spool down from 15,000 rpm. The attitude indicators started to bounce and jump around a bit as they always do on shut off. My relief was palpable.

The distorting look of total fear just seconds after shutting down the oil-deprived "Spirit of San Diego" on the tarmac at Kuala Lumpur International 2 as rescue vehicles quickly approach…

Emergency crews and vehicles with their lights flashing started to park around my plane. It was not on fire. I expected to see steam or smoke coming off it, but there was nothing. The cockpit was a shambles with red plastic oil bottles, black tops, a black plastic bag and small Malaysian flag on a wooden stick between the seats. I reached down to the seat next to me and grabbed my cell phone and recorded myself describing what had just happened to me. I was the face of fear and survival.

I unbuckled my safety belts. My legs and hands were trembling; I was taking short breaths and could smell the perspiration that covered me. I was in a daze and having a hard time comprehending everything that had just happened. Getting up I went to open the hatch. As the top half of the clamshell hatch opened I could hear the hydraulic shock absorber slow its movement and make a hiss while the door reached full extension. A rush of warm humid air flowed into the pressurized cabin. It smelled like jet exhaust from the commercial planes that were taking off around me. The people who had rushed in from the rescue crew surrounded the plane. A man with a yellow reflective vest with the words "AVSEC" on it for aviation security was the first to get to me. He asked me from just outside the cockpit window with a frantic and scared Malaysian accent, "Are you okay?"

"The Spirit of San Diego" hemorrhaging hot black oil after the
engine is hastily shut down.

None of us knew what would happen next. Certainly we were all thinking that the plane could in fact burst into flames. What they could see that I could not, was that hot black oil was dripping from the plane's cowling, the covering of the engine. The oil had more than likely made it past the super-heated 1500 degree exhaust and turbo chargers. I lifted the lever on the bottom hatch, pulled the cable until it was taut and began to let the bottom half of the clamshell door down. The emergency crew helped me out and we got some distance between us and the plane. Again they asked, "Are you sure you are okay, do you need medical attention?"

I was visibly shaken and the only answer I could get out seemed to trickle out of my mouth was, "I'm alive, I'm okay."

I had question after question rolling through my mind. One of which was how and why was I alive? I didn't know whether to be angry and curse God or be thankful. What about my plane? Did the *Spirit of San Diego* just betray me in the most dramatic and public of ways or save my life? How would this affect the rest of the trip? And, of course, what should I learn from this? Was this the signal to give up and go home or was I just provided with a fascinating and dramatic story I could lecture and write about for the next thirty years? I didn't know, except that it all had just unfolded exactly as it was intended to and for a reason.

The sooner I could learn the reason and lesson behind this near disaster I could understand what I must do to move on and not have to go through this ever again. I knew the universe taught me its lessons in this way, like a loving parent trying to teach a child. At first the lesson was delivered in a gentle fashion. If it went unheeded, the lesson was taught again with more intensity. And it would continue until learning took place. The parent would never give up on such an important lesson. It showed the child was loved beyond measure. The parent and the Universe were both teachers with enough lessons to last a lifetime and perhaps beyond.

In that moment, my understanding of the concept of gratitude deepened. I was thankful for every breath I took, for each beat of my heart and every movement of my body. I was thankful that I would see and talk to my family and friends again and thankful above all else to be on the ground with the *Spirit of San Diego*. I had been tested under the most extreme pressure a pilot can face and survived. In my mind I had pulled off the impossible.

This ten-minute test was finally over after what seemed like an eternity. I hoped that I would never be tested like this again, but I still had an uneasy feeling in my stomach that there would be more. I knew that gifts sometimes come in the form of lessons. Was this lesson to prepare me for something ahead? My world had been turned upside down and I knew this was far from over.

I would later discover that this had happened because the oil hose from inside the cockpit, designed to put oil in the engine in flight from the pressurized cabin, had broken off on the side of the engine where it connected to the oil drain line. The part that separated appeared to be twisted in half. The cost of this part was about one dollar. It was shocking to me that a one-dollar part could bring down this half-million dollar aircraft. The supplemental oil system was intended to replenish the vital engine oil that would burn off during the long flights, not drain the oil out in twenty minutes.

There were two theories on what had caused this part to separate. The mechanic in Malaysia that changed the oil and cleaned the spark plugs was convinced that the weight of the fitting from the supplemental oil system vibrating over the last one hundred hours was the source of the problem. He believed that the weight of the assembly was too heavy and should have been made out of aluminum. The assembly was indeed heavy and it seemed like a plausible explanation.

The second explanation was that while removing and reinstalling the spark plugs, one of the mechanics broke off the oil fitting. This seemed more likely to me as the plane had worked perfectly until the work had been done and failed immediately afterwards.

As I think back to the mechanics' work on the plane, I remember watching from the corner of my eye while having a conversation with a television reporter and seeing something that did not make sense to me. I saw how the lead mechanic leaned heavily with all his weight to tighten the spark plugs. He didn't grip the wrench at the socket with one hand but rather put both hands on the end of the wrench, which could have created a sheering effect. My intuition had given me a sign, but it didn't register and I chose to ignore it, assuming that an experienced mechanic would know better than me. The pilot is ultimately responsible for his plane. That small detail could have cost me my life.

Cleaning plugs is a relatively simple job but without the care of a mother holding her newborn, it could be a death sentence. This aircraft was high performance, yes, but it was high maintenance as well.

Thoughts raced through my mind filled with more questions. Could my greatest passion also lead to my demise? What would be the point in that? Did I need to have an accident to fulfill my goal of teaching pilots about pilot safety? I wanted to be an example, but this was beyond what I was signing up for. To teach others would I have to experience this first hand?

Those who are familiar with aircraft will tell you that it sometimes takes many hours to spot problems in an engine. Annual inspections are painfully detailed and can take several days to perform. Mechanics use small mirrors to see around things that would be impossible to spot with the naked eye. Would a pilot not trained in aircraft repair be able to spot what was not obvious to a number of trained mechanics?

An additional factor that led me to believe the problem resulted from the mechanics' over-torquing the oil fitting came to me as I watched them attempt to remove the fitting by applying too much force, which actually broke the head on the right front cylinder. Eventually we were able to remove the fitting and slow the leak in the head with high temperature epoxy long enough for me to fly the plane back to the repair facility in Subang. While the leak had not been completely stopped, it slowed enough to retain some engine oil during the twenty-minute flight.

The sheared $1 oil fitting from the oil drain line on the right top
cylinder of the "Spirit of San Diego" that brought her down less than
20 minutes after takeoff from Kuala Lumpur International 2.

The phrase "hanger rash" is used to describe
what happens to a plane when it is damaged while

under the care of a mechanic. Planes get bumped and broken in the process of trying to fix them. Think of a child picking up a delicate butterfly to play with; their little hands can easily damage the wings of this miraculous flying creature. Mechanics, like children, do not intentionally harm a plane, but it does happen regularly.

Zen Moment

The sooner I could learn the reason and lesson behind this near disaster, I could understand what I must do to move on and not have to go through this ever again. I knew the universe taught me its lessons in this way, like a loving parent trying to teach a child.

Zen Moment

In the moment following my harrowing landing, I would deepen my understanding of the concept of gratitude. I was thankful for each breath I took, for each beat of my heart and every movement of my body. I was thankful that I would see and talk to my family and friends again and thankful above all else to be on the ground. I had been tested under the most extreme pressure a pilot can face and survived. In my mind I had pulled off the impossible.

Zen Moment

I hated the Universe in this moment and wondered if I had done something to deserve this. Little did I know I was in the hands of God about to be taught one of the most valuable lessons of my life. I looked out at each side of the forty-three-foot wingspan and thought to myself, I'm landing on angel wings," and everything seemed to turn into slow motion. For a second, I was weightless and floating. Everybody who had followed me was holding me up. My mother who had passed years before, my family and friends, my sponsors and all the people whose names I didn't even know that were watching. I was on the wings of love.

Chapter 15

In the Spotlight

Over the next few days that mechanics needed to repair the aircraft, hundreds of people that worked at the airport came around to see it. Few people in Malaysia had seen a small aircraft and certainly none that looked as sexy as the *Spirit of San Diego* with her twenty-three flags up both sides as well as her thirty-five different color sponsor logos. The plane was indeed special and you could see that from the HF antenna that went from the pilot window to the tip of the left wing and then back to the tail. She looked like she could take on the world … and she was doing exactly that.

Many of the people who greeted me as we worked on the plane had questions about the flight. It seemed that word about the dramatic emergency landing that had disrupted the flow of commercial traffic spread quickly around the airport. Kuala Lumpur International 2 is the second smaller airport in Kuala Lumpur. It's the low-cost hub with nothing larger that 737s flying in and out all day. The people I met expressed support for me and I have to admit, for a time I felt a little larger than life. On my departure, I received gifts of food and a signature shirt and ball cap along with many wishes for safety on my flight ahead.

Fruit given upon departure from Malaysia

Even the vice president of AirAsia had asked to meet me, and eventually Malaysia Airports asked if I would put their logo on my plane. They had been so generous to me with respect to the emergency service they provided and the daily support as we repaired the plane on the tarmac, I was happy to put the decal on the *Spirit of San Diego*, making them my thirty-sixth sponsor. I felt a real sense of compassion from the people at the airport and it was an honor to have met them.

I was so focused on each leg I had really lost track of what I was doing overall. It takes almost laser focus to keep the details of a trip this complicated under control. I had to eat the elephant one bite at a time or it would be over-whelming. If I didn't care about making an impact on the world and was just flying instead, it would have been much easier. But with all the components, including social media, branding, public relations, sponsorship, books, blogs and articles, it became an enormous undertaking and responsibility. One of the most recent earthrounders spent over ten thousand dollars a month on PR alone for the twelve months prior to the trip and three months after. Our goal was not for profit and we were able to accomplish much of the same thing on a shoestring budget.

I had been sitting for almost an hour in an office in Malaysia at the SAS repair facility waiting for my second flight plan to clear. The tower wasn't able to find my first flight plan, which led me to a discussion with two regional pilots about whether the local air traffic controllers and tower operators cared at all about the smaller general aviation aircraft they were directing. Before I could even plead my case with the dramatic story of the controllers trying to direct my damaged plane back to my departure airport, which was beyond my glide range and would have resulted in a ditching in the jungle or Strait of Malacca, they both blurted out in unison, "No, not at all." It's an unusual moment in time when three pilots can all agree on the same thing. I thought perhaps I had been a little dramatic, but I found these professional pilots confirmed what I had long thought.

Looking back to my brief five-year flying career I considered a few close calls I had in other parts of the world that could have potentially been fatal. There was the experience in Istanbul when, as I attempted to land, the controller tried four times to direct me into a storm that would have brought down my plane. Or the Puerto Rican air traffic controller who got confused and instructed me to turn left into a mountain rather than right while I was in the clouds. While I believe the air traffic controllers in both of these situations were well intentioned, I accepted that I could not rely on any of their recommendations without first carefully evaluating what they had told me.

In that moment, it hit me so hard it almost knocked me over: I was connecting the dots on all the uncertainty with my trip, which led me to wonder what I could really have faith in. I still faced flying over ten thousand nautical miles of mostly open ocean to complete the trip.

Letting go of control in Malaysia

The *Spirit of San Diego* had been parked on the tarmac in Malaysia with full fuel and fresh oil for just over ten days. There had been no thunder of her twin turbo-charged engine, no climbing through endless layers of cirrus clouds, no sweet female computer voice warning me of traffic or terrain and no sound as the landing gear folds inward and upward to form a seamless seal against the undercarriage of the plane.

I was literally grounded and it was beyond my control.

I had been patiently waiting for a permit to either land or overfly Indonesia on my way to the Australian continent. The reasons from the Indonesian Civilian Airport Authority (CAA) for the delay changed daily and ranged from "volcanic activity," "a religious holiday," "we are too busy," "get back to you later" and "the office is closed."

Now, my plane can fly at twenty-five thousand feet, which is twelve thousand feet above the highest level of ash. Furthermore, commercial flights were going in and out every five minutes. This gave me an excellent opportunity to practice patience, one of my life lessons and clearly where I have more work to do.

On a deeper level, I believed I was meant to learn something more before I could move forward on my trip. My life was being slowed down and it was beyond my control. I made the best of my delay by flying commercially to Chiang Mai in Thailand, and Vientiane and Luang Prabang in Laos.

In these places, I saw great beauty in the waterfalls, mountains and rivers. I tried many types of healthy and delicious food.

I laughed and joked with people from many different countries that I never would have seen as friends. I rode on the neck of a trumpeting elephant across a river.

Eating healthy fresh food in the open air market in Laos for just $1.50 a meal

Feeding a gentle giant that trumpeted as I rode on his neck

During that time, I sat and talked with a Buddhist monk on a mountaintop and prayed with another at a temple.

Having a conversation about life with a teenaged Buddhist Monk on a mountaintop in Laos proved enlightening.

I began to see I had been missing the texture of life by focusing on each destination and not the lessons or experiences I could have along the way.

The Universe was slowing me down and reminding me that the reward and learning was in the time in between on the journey. I was reminded that this flight, this adventure, was not about the record it would set but rather about the record of interactions that are imprinted on me and what I will take forward and do with them. The time in between is the richest, most sacred of all.

Zen Moment

I began to see I was missing the texture of life by focusing on each destination and not the lessons or experiences I could have along the way. The Universe was slowing me down and reminding me that the reward and learning was in the time in between on the journey.

Zen Moment

I was reminded that this flight, this adventure, was not about the record it would set but rather about the record of interactions that are imprinted on me and what I will take forward and do with them. The time in between is the richest, most sacred of all.

Chapter 16

Zen Test Pilot

After proper repairing of the oil fitting and waiting twenty-four hours for the epoxy to cure, it was time for someone to test fly the *Spirit of San Diego*. The problem was that after my engine failed over the Strait of Malacca, the last thing in the world I wanted to do was get back into a plane that had nearly taken my life. I couldn't establish what damage had been done to the plane engine internally, like wondering what had happened inside a box that you couldn't see into. The thought of two turbochargers spinning at 90,000 rpm each without oil and hundreds of mechanical parts moving as the engine wind milled at 2,750 rpm and zero oil pressure for up to five minutes made my stomach turn.

Still, it was clear that the person who was going to test fly the plane was me. Nobody I had come across in Malaysia had any experience flying a Malibu Mirage, and I couldn't help but wonder if anyone in his right mind would even want to fly a plane that had experienced zero oil pressure. All pilots at some point are called on to become test pilots. Every time a new part goes into a plane there is a risk as aircraft parts typically fail during the first 10 percent and last 10 percent of their lives. And engines typically fail on takeoff or landing as mine did. So adding up the probabilities about what can happen when a plane has been worked on in a repair facility, its pilot has entered the ranks of the test pilot!

Many people I respected were giving me information that was all contradictory. Some suggested the option of shipping the six hundred-hour engine I had back in the states to Malaysia to have it installed. I didn't know the history on this engine and I still had the install issue.

I didn't want the previous mechanics to be involved since they had almost just killed me while doing minor work and did not know the Lycoming IO-540 engine. The installation of an aircraft engine is complex and I needed an expert I could trust with my life.

I found another mechanic who had some experience maintaining several helicopters that used a similar Lycoming IO-540, but they were not turbo charged. To add insult to injury, the mechanic didn't speak English and didn't seem very interested in my project.

The cost of flying a mechanic out for a week with a new or six hundred-hour engine would be enormous. Was the devil that I knew (the installed engine) better than the devil I did not know (the new engine)? And one set of eyes on an engine install was not enough to have 100 percent confidence. So the million-dollar question was how do I fly the *Spirit of San Diego* another ten- to fourteen thousand nautical miles, over the water at twenty-three thousand feet, when I had lost confidence in the engine?

I arrived at a solution after conversations with Susan Gilbert, a friend, mentor, my angel, the brains behind my branding, digital and social media marketing and books, owner of Online Promotion Success and former pilot who was with me for three weeks in Europe. She suggested I go with the person who knew the engine the best. That was my mechanic back home, Dan Salzman from High Performance Aircraft. After an enormous number of checks on the engine, he suggested that I test fly it until I had enough confidence to go on to my next destination of Jakarta, Indonesia. The archipelago of Indonesia is composed of a series of islands with airports scattered along the island chain as well as an active volcano, which was erupting at the time.

One mechanic I trusted who had earned a reputation as an expert in the community was Chad Menne from Malibu Aerospace, also in the states. Chad told me that the turbochargers may appear fine now, but they could fail in another ten to twenty hours, which would have put me in the Indian Ocean or Coral Sea, hundreds of miles off the shark-infested coast of Australia. After my return to the US, Chad saw me present at the Malibu Mirage Owners Pilot Association (MMOPA) and, with his great sense of humor, said, "I really meant to say ten to thirty hours." I wondered if that was humor only I and the others who had done flights like this could appreciate.

The plan in action

My intended solution was to fly a racetrack pattern ten thousand feet over Subang International for several hours until I was satisfied with the performance of the engine. I figured if the engine failed I could do a spiral down and land on its long 12,402-foot runway. This request seemed to totally confuse the air traffic controllers and I waited in the run-up area for thirty minutes while they tried to figure out what to do with me.

Eventually they came up with a plan to send me out over the Strait of Malacca to test my engine at five hundred feet above the water. This was an extremely dangerous place to test an engine as it would give me virtually no time to recover if the engine failed. I would be in the water seconds later. After playing along with the insanity for a forty-five-minute flight, I decided it was infinitely better to continue on my trip and fly along the island chains of Indonesia at altitude rather than risk this low-level flight over the water.

Eddie at GASE had charted out all possible landing spots for me on the way to Indonesia and done calculations to determine how often I would be outside the gliding range of the aircraft. He agreed that this was a better option for me.

The following day as I prepared for my departure/test flight I found getting back into that plane to be very challenging. I was having flashbacks to the moment the oil light went on, the propeller oversped, the warning lights going off and my arguing with the air traffic controllers. If ever I had to draw on my inner strength to keep going after what I had dealt with, this was that moment.

I closed my eyes for a brief second and asked for some guidance and not another cosmic ass whooping. What came to me was surprising: It was that in fact the plane had saved me, not nearly taken my life. I was reminded that the plane did not catch on fire with the oil dripping on the 1,500-degree exhaust; the oil had not blown on the windshield and blocked my view; the landing gear had held despite the enormous weight it was not designed to handle on landing; the engine had not seized or been damaged; the plane was not destroyed; I was within gliding distance of the airport despite the enormous drag created by the wind milling propeller, and, oh, by the way, I was in one piece and this very same plane was going to fly me home.

All these things in combination defied logic. Nobody could come up with a rational explanation of why I was still alive. It added to my belief that all that had happened was for a purpose much bigger than what I could conceive at the time. I was certainly being guided and protected. I had no idea how many more times on this trip this would be proven to me. For now, though, I knew I was on the right path and being protected, guided and taught. I was being compelled to continue on my journey. I would like to say at that point my fear went away, but it did not. I continued to doubt myself, my plane and God. Apparently I would need more signs to have total faith.

During the second day of flight on my way to Darwin, Australia from Indonesia, I decided to fly up at twenty-five thousand feet versus my usual twenty-one thousand feet. The weather was bad and I hoped to avoid it and that the extra four thousand feet would give me more gliding distance should I have another engine out. However, flying this high meant that I was working the turbochargers hotter than usual. This concerned me in that I wanted to go easy on them after the engine failure. But I made the deliberate decision to do so, given the need to go above the bad weather rather than slug it out at a lower altitude. Being able to get above the weather was the great advantage of turbocharging, but I was nervous as I had no way of really knowing the condition of my turbo chargers.

I was finally starting to calm down on this flight and I figured I was getting past all this drama. It was time to do a routine shifting of the fuel tank from the 140-gallon interior ferry tank back to the left main wing tank. This time I wanted to make it happen seamlessly. I got the light flicker on the fuel pressure warning light, the engine sputtered and I turned on the fuel pump and then, using the fuel selector switch, switched the tanks.

At that point, instead of the engine catching again, the prop instantly oversped just as it had on my engine out. It sounded as if the prop had instantly doubled its speed. The engine was pushing past redline, not a place it liked to be. I was expecting a loud explosion once again as the engine was about to blow itself apart. No way could it run at this speed for very long. It was turning much faster than it was designed. This had me totally confused as the system that controlled the pitch on propeller was totally unrelated to the fuel. It was in fact oil that controlled the pitch of the propeller.

I found that this and every subsequent in-flight emergency I experienced would have nearly the same effect on me that the loss of engine oil pressure had over the Strait of Malacca. My stomach went to my throat; I felt panic, loss of breath, perspiration, sense of doom, imminent death, confusion and self-doubt. Was this what post-traumatic stress felt like?

I handled it as I did before, starting with a "Shit no!" I regained my composure, throttled back, and pulled the prop back, which responded this time because the engine still had oil in it.

The most confusing part of this was that when I asked my mechanic about the cause of the over speed there was a long pause. This didn't make sense. I called another mechanic and got the same long pause. The closest thing to an answer that we could come up with was that the high altitude somehow played a role. They were totally unrelated systems and there was no logical connection. This was one of those situations that nobody could explain and that, fortunately, would never happen again.

I was concerned that there was damage to the prop when it has lost oil and the entire system was breaking down. By this time in the trip, I was in a state of high stress and now I could add my propeller to the list of equipment I no longer trusted. It was as if the plane was not happy being put through this series of strenuous events and, like a child, throwing a temper tantrum to let me know it was in control. I was merely along for the ride. I'd have to endure the backlash and hope that this angry child would continue to play along in this game of life and death.

Zen Moment

I closed my eyes for a brief second and asked for some guidance and not another cosmic ass whooping. What came to me was surprising. It was that in fact the plane had saved me not nearly taken my life.

Zen Moment

All these things in combination defied logic. Nobody could come up with a rational explanation of why I was still alive. It added to my belief that all that had happened was for a purpose much bigger than what I could conceive at the time. I was certainly being guided and protected. I had no idea how many more times on this trip this would be proven to me. For now, though, I knew I was on the right path and being protected, guided and taught. I was being compelled to continue on my journey. I would like to say at that point my fear went away, but it did not. I continued to doubt myself, my plane and God. Apparently I would need more signs to have total faith.

Chapter 17

Night Over the Pacific

My numerous delays had once again put me over the Pacific at night. As I headed into American Samoa from Noumea, New Caledonia my stomach was churning and I wasn't sure why, though it was a damn scary place to be in the absolutely pitch black of the Pacific. I looked out the left cockpit window and thought it couldn't be much darker if I had closed my eyes. Surely there must be something out there to make some light—a ship, another plane, a firefly or maybe some bioluminescence? The Universe responded by saying, "No light out there, nothing at all." Not very inviting and certainly not the glorious call to adventure I had envisioned.

I was about one hundred nautical miles out from American Samoa and was anticipating something coming up. My intuition was going off, and I felt this wasn't going to be a feel-good moment. I was starting to dial in my landing frequencies, looking at the approach charts, making my notations and thinking how dimly lit the cockpit was —sort of an orange-brown glow and definitely not cheerful. I felt a wave of panic come over me, wondering to myself, *how did I get myself into this shitty situation?* Certainly I had not thought through the moment of being alone, twenty-one thousand high in the total darkness of night over the Pacific.

The reality was this would prove to be one of my most difficult landings of the trip. I would have to deal with heavy turbulence, penetrate a low cloud layer, mountains on both sides of the runway, gusting twenty-knot winds, an uncontrolled tower with pilot-activated lights and a handoff from Approach Control to a non-towered airport. That was not a good combination of things to be happening in a short period of time. I remember asking myself, "Are you up for this?" I was not having a rah-rah moment in which I felt like I could do anything. Instead I was thinking I'm tired, this flight was longer and more fatiguing than I expected. The answer that came back was the wrong answer: "No, I am not ready for this moment."

As I got closer to American Samoa and had descended to about twelve thousand feet I would again hear from the air traffic controller. What chilled me was that when she spoke to me on the HF radio it sounded as if she had dialed me up from the underworld. As if I was the next soul she was coming to claim and she almost had me.

Her tone had a certain loathing and general lack of concern. She seemed annoyed that she even had to talk to me. When I was about twenty nautical miles from the airport and descending at over 200 mph she said in a slow and almost morbid fashion, "November Niner Niner Seven Mike Alpha, laaaaand at yourrrr oooooown risk." Then the silent hiss of the HF radio. *Hisssss.* Like the underworld had taken her back and she would be waiting, laughing at what a fool I was. Her words seemed to communicate, "You are crazy for even trying this at night in the middle of the Pacific." *You deserve whatever happens to you ... you idiot. What a welcome*, I thought...

I wasn't sure what was worse, being alone in the darkness at that point or talking to this dark creature from the underworld.

I would be forced to call her back a second time to help me locate the frequency for the tower-controlled lighting. As luck would have it the only other flight that would land on the island that week was an hour behind me and had the frequency. It was like I was in the midst of this cosmic shit storm and the gods decided to throw me a bone as if to keep this drama going as long as they could for their entertainment. Or were they pulling for me? I didn't know. It seemed to me that I was engaged in an epic struggle.

Beginning my descent through the cloud layer, I was violently tossed around in the turbulence that stressed my plane. I could see the strobe lights' reflection off the clouds that were hitting the windshield at over 200 mph. Time started to slow and I looked over at the empty seat to my right. It was lit by the eerie glow of the flight instruments and very empty. I was in this alone with my close friend fear in my little twisted version of reality. My own little shop of horrors.

What was the series of events that had led me to this point in my life where I would take such incredible risks? I was so glad I was not subjecting another soul to this abuse. That would have been reckless of me. I looked out and saw the wings flexing and then heard a thunderous *booooooooom!* It was the ferry tank explosively equalizing pressure behind me. My stomach didn't just go to my throat it went out my mouth that time. *Why does this need to be so fucking hard?* I thought. I could feel the relentless pull of the underworld.

The violent pounding of the aircraft continued for another twenty seconds and then I broke out of the clouds. I could see the ten thousand-foot runway lit up like a Christmas tree. The wind I was now feeling was shooting over the mountains from my left and accelerating. I was pushing my right rudder pedal as hard as I could to straighten out the aircraft. There was no more correction possible. I had the rudder pedal all the way to the cabin bulkhead. The plane was at its limit and I was at my limit. We were both being tested.

Like the loyal horse that follows its rider into battle with no idea what the consequences of its actions will be, the *Spirit of San Diego* was doing everything I asked of her. As I lined up on the runway, I realized I just needed to stay focused for a few more seconds. This test is almost over. As the mains touched down I felt my soul reconnect with the earth. The energy I was carrying released from my body like a Fourth of July fountain of sparks shooting into the air and I felt an enormous sense of release. I was so happy to be alive. I had not been taken. I had fought well and won.

The handler who met me knew all the details of this small island. He was Caucasian but spoke like an islander and assured me I was in good hands as he had helped many pilots before me. I did not have the required customs and immigration documents from my previous stop in Noumea, New Caledonia, due to a last-minute administrative issue that delayed me. My handler smiled with a sly grin and let me know he could handle that as well.

A frightening energy

The four days I stayed on Pago Pago, the capital of American Samoa—a cluster of tiny islands in the middle of the Pacific and two thousand nautical miles from any real form of civilization—were frightening for me. It's hard to describe, but the feel of the island made my skin crawl. Imagine a tribal culture that somehow was rapidly updated with some American infrastructure with cell phones, an airport, McDonald's and sketchy Internet. But beyond that, it felt like the people were still driven by thousands of years of tribal tradition, like they didn't really want any of the new lifestyle that had been thrust upon them. And for that matter, they could do without the occasional visitors as well. Civilized man had made an attempt to tame the island, but what mattered to civilized man didn't appeal to the locals. They would just as soon sit on their porches eating off the land and living out their lives.

Beyond that, to me American Samoa felt as if it represented some substantial energetic barrier. This place wasn't going to make it easy on you. It was going to throw some serious challenges your way and if you weren't strong enough, smart enough or clever enough, this was going to be your last stop. In a way, in the middle of the ocean you really were quite inconsequential. Nature seemed to be the predominant force.

I couldn't shake the tragic story of seventeen-year-old Haris Suleman and his father, Babar, American-Pakistani pilots who were circumnavigating the world in 2014 with Haris at the helm. They were taking off from American Samoa but violently crashed into the water just a mile off the end of the runway. Both were killed and the father's body was never found. I didn't understand why they couldn't locate it, given that the runway is so close to the ocean until I sat on a beach watching the waves slam with tremendous force against the shoreline. Immense white-capped waves, sea mist, cold water. It was like looking into the mouth of a demon. This place was dead serious and I wasn't looking forward to my test. Not to mention how I could still sense the father and son's energy and I knew the father's body was somewhere out there; I could feel it. It reminded me of a passage from Charles Lindbergh's *The Spirit of St. Louis*:

> *"It's a fierce, unfriendly sea—a sea that would batter the largest ocean liner. I feel naked above it, as though stripped of all protection, conscious of the terrific strength of the waves, of the thinness of cloth on my wings, of the dark turbulence of the storm clouds. This would be a hellish place to land if the engine failed."*

While walking around the island I had the recurring thought that the island would claim all the planes that would dare to make the journey. Had I honored the gods or offended them? Would my purpose be to act as a warning to wealthy pilots all over the world that were allowing their egos to drive them to their deaths? How many lives could this island take and was I strong enough to continue on and finish this trip?

In my mind it would be so easy to give up, but I was committed. Quitting was not an option. I was on the path that Spirit had for me even if that meant that the path I was on was getting me closer to my final moments in this life.

All these things resulted in confused and conflicted feelings while I was on the island. My sleep suffered, which made the situation worse. I really needed to be in top form to deal with these life-or-death situations, but I was finding myself waking up around 2:00 a.m., lying in a pool of sweat and having a severe panic attack. If I were to give the feelings I was having a voice, my inner child was crying and shouting, *I'm scared! Why are you doing this to me? Why are you putting us into this dangerous situation where we could die? This was supposed to be fun like in Europe. I want to go home!* My job was always to support him and not put him at extreme risk.

I kept having visions of ditching in the open ocean and watching the plane fill up with water. I was desperately trying to *not* manifest that outcome and be called to live my greatest fear.

While I was in American Samoa Eddie asked me if I would release some flowers into the ocean to honor the Sulemans. I would be the first to complete the round-the-world flight since their tragic end.

Their story haunted me and I couldn't help but replay it in my mind constantly. I was judging them (and as a result me) rather than focusing my energy on my trip and my survival. I hoped their souls were resting peacefully and was trying to learn the lesson that the Universe had provided to us all.

I did a tribute to them one morning on the beach at the hotel where they had also stayed. I collected bright orange and red tropical flowers from different local trees and bushes. The flowers were each the size of a hand and looked like a dancer might wear them in her hair at a luau. The center of the flowers had delicate long white stamens that looked like eyelashes.

One of the flowers that I sent out to sea to honor the Sulemans who died on takeoff from Pago Pago.

I commended the Sulemans for pursuing their passions, for taking a chance at something bigger than themselves and for dreaming impossibly big. I was overcome with emotion in that moment and their experience seemed too close to home for me. I cried afterward as I watched the current take the flowers out to sea. That island held an enormous amount of energy related to their passing and I was having serious doubts if I would be allowed to leave.

My approach into American Samoa had been one of my most challenging nighttime instrument approaches of my life. Everything I was gaining on the island was not coming easily. It felt like I was fighting just to remain there. Nature was very raw and I had this sense that the island wanted to be left alone and would swallow up all those that wandered in uninvited.

Zen Moment

Quitting was not an option. I was on the path that Spirit had for me even if that meant that the path I was on was getting me closer to my final moments in this life.

Chapter 18

Departing American Samoa

My near-critical mistake would eventually come on takeoff out of American Samoa. A few days before, I had landed on Runway 5/23, the ten thousand-foot runway in Pago Pago, arriving in from the ocean. I believed that with favorable wind conditions, I would take off from the same runway in the opposite direction out over the ocean, giving me the long roll I desperately needed. I wouldn't have terrain to clear, which was good since I was flying the plane very heavy.

Pago Pago also has a much shorter cross-runway, Runway 08/26, that also puts you over the ocean. But that runway was technically too short for my plane with its more than 10 percent over max gross weight. The pilot-operating handbook doesn't give details about takeoff performance when flying 10 percent over max gross, but as you might imagine, it's going to take considerable runway to make that happen.

Just prior to start up, I was doing my preflight and I noticed the engine only had five quarts of oil in it from my earlier leg from Noumea. Eleven quarts was the recommended oil level, and now I realized that my plane had burned six quarts of oil during the eight-hour flight! That was an enormous amount of oil to burn in one flight. I felt my stomach turn and my body heat start to rise. I was screwed and there was nobody on this entire island that could do a thing for me. Likely no one had heard of a Malibu Mirage and I certainly didn't trust anybody to put a hand on the *Spirit of San Diego* after what had happened in Malaysia.

I put six quarts into the engine, wondering as I did so if the ground crew noticed that I was putting in such a huge amount. I rationalized that I was still above one quart an hour, but this was not what I wanted to be burning over my next leg to Kiribati, which was even more remote and wouldn't have oil for me to purchase. Worse yet, what if I had burned the six quarts in the last hour? Perhaps one of the oil rings had just let go in the final moments of the trip and I was intended to find this out and not continue. A deep sense of doom came over me.

I noted a lack of eye contact from the ground staff, the same thing I observed from the lead mechanic when I departed Subang, Malaysia minutes before my engine out over the Strait of Malacca. My stomach was once again churning, a feeling I knew well. I was sweating and I had a sense that I had another extreme lesson on the way. I was tired of these terrifying lessons, which never seemed to end. The ground crew looked depressed and sad and my sense was they were thinking how I was the first to attempt the around-the-world flight since the Sulemans. Indeed, the entire island knew the story and my departure was bringing up feelings in all of them as well.

Why did this have to be so f'ing difficult? I wondered if I was really controlling my reality or was this fate? Was I mechanically progressing toward an outcome I could not avoid? Were my forty-nine years of life meant to end on the islands of American Samoa? Was that my contract with the Universe? And if so why put me through all this stress? Just take me quickly. Why did the Universe appear so cruel at times?

A seemingly insignificant encounter with a crab on one of the Pacific islands demonstrated to me how cruel the Universe can be and that we are all insignificant in the grand scheme of things. One night I was trying to leave my room without turning on the light to avoid attracting mosquitoes and other miniature monsters. As I walked out the front door, I could hear a crackling on the floor; it sounded like loose linoleum that had been put down in a hurry on a surface to which it couldn't stick. I didn't give it much thought at the time.

When I returned to the room later that night I thought it wise to check the room, which I did routinely as a precaution on entering a new hotel room. I started with the dark little bathroom with the tattletale-grey towels with frayed edges and holes; next I gripped the closest door, which I noted had to be hollow since it felt like I could lift it off the hinges if I had the slightest desire. Then I got down on my hands and knees to look under the bed.

As my vision came into focus I instinctively jumped a foot and let out a "Holy shit." I was face to face with a full-sized crab under my bed. As I jumped, he ran towards me in a show of force. I leaped out of the way, my heart beating a freaking nautical mile a minute as I stared at this little monster. He was staring back at me, with his one oversized left claw up in the air ready to do battle. I could see that this was not his first fight since his second claw was much smaller and in the process of growing back. I looked at him eye to eye. His eyes were attached at the end of small protrusions from his body and they were dancing about. I thought he had some big balls for a little guy as he sized me up. I would have thought he would fall back, hide and fight another day, but, no, this guy was a warrior.

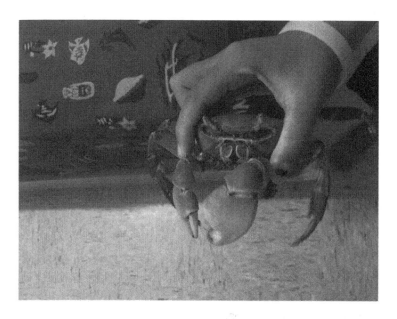

A fearless crab found tap dancing under my bed and ready for battle on the Island of Kiribati in the Tarawa island chain.

I immediately asked for assistance of the front-desk clerk who seemed adept at removing monsters from under beds. The front-desk clerk, a local girl aged twenty, sighed when she saw him, like a parent spotting the mess his or her child has made and left all over the floor. Clearly put out by having to deal with this sort of situation, she cornered the crab, grabbing him from above and behind with a swift and well-rehearsed movement.

The clerk smiled and then apologized for what she could not control. Before she started to walk out I motioned that she stage him for his first selfie. As she held him up to my phone he was motionless, seeming to accept his fate as an "Internet superstar." I had the shot in a second and she walked outside and tossed the crab into a fifty-five-gallon oil drum in the common area.

I heard the *thud* as he hit the side of the drum, as though she were tossing out a can of soda. I thought that was not a very heroic end for such a brave little warrior. Surely he deserved better, but maybe that was how the Universe handled the end for some after the fight of their lives? Just a *thud* and then it was over. The Universe could be cruel.

It occurred to me that people were the visitors and nature was an ever-present force that was trying to reclaim what was always hers. It was a struggle that would continue as long as we were here.

Ready for takeoff

I snapped back to reality when the handler asked me, "On which runway would you like to depart?"

I said, "The one that puts me over the ocean," thinking of the ten thousand-foot one I had come in on, Runway 05/23. I had quite forgotten that the short runway did as well. The handler looked down and away and pointed me in the direction of the shorter runway like he couldn't bear to see the outcome of what was about to happen next although he was unaware of the distance my plane desperately needed for a safe departure. I thought I was taking the longer runway and was about to roll the dice for the fifth time on my trip with nobody but me playing in this game.

At that moment, I was distracted and busy questioning my decision to fly the plane with what appeared to be a rough running right magneto, one of the two electrical systems that supply current to the spark plugs. The magneto seemed to be fine at altitude but at 2,000 rpm during run up they were having issues. The engine sputtered and popped a few times as if daring me to proceed. I wondered if the ground crew heard that and would report it if my flight ended like the Sulemans' did. I felt a twinge of embarrassment for even proceeding. My manifold pressure was also a couple inches low, which was important for developing full horsepower during the takeoff roll. I had been carefully weighing the decision of having someone who had absolutely no aviation experience take a look at the engine or waiting until two legs later in Hawaii where I had confidence in the service I would receive.

I no longer had confidence in foreign mechanics, having felt they had brought me the nearest to death on my trip. I was also weighing the option of an additional one- to-two-week delay and flying a mechanic in with Piper experience from the US at great expense. None of these options was ideal or without risks.

Then again, my trip was certainly not ideal or without risks. I had been living with this stress now for almost two-and-a-half months. I was at least in a place with the word "America" in it. I was getting closer to home. Only the mighty Pacific lay between me and San Diego. I had been tested so many times by this point, I was tired and wondered if I was strong enough to complete this trip. My inner child was right; it was time to go home.

It was a rainy, misty and shitty marginal-visibility day, leaving me unable to see the end of the runway. I could see that the ocean was rough with foam and white caps. It looked like it would be difficult even for a large ship to make it through those waters. I kept thinking that Babar Suleman was still floating around out there, claimed and swallowed up by the Pacific Ocean. It felt like a graveyard eager for its next victim.

I was happy to be leaving American Samoa and that unsettling energy behind me. I remember gently pushing the throttle, propeller and fuel control forward, it was a white knuckle moment and my knees would have been shaking if I hadn't been busy applying hard right rudder to counteract the takeoff forces as I sped down the runway.

I watched the speed slowly increase under the enormous fuel load. Thirty knots and then thirty-five. The plane was making only thirty-nine inches of manifold pressure, which equated to power. The number I was used to was forty-three inches. Forty knots, 45 knots. I needed 85 knots to rotate. The plane pulled a bit to left under the torque of the engine and I quickly corrected. Passing 60 knots. I still had minimally another 25 knots of speed before I could rotate. It was at that point I could begin to see a figure start to take shape out of the fog in the distance. Seventy knots. The figure was several feet high and seemed to go the entire width of the runway!

Holy shit, it was a fence! I was only a third of the way down the runway, so how was that possible? Suddenly it hit me—the handler had put me on the shorter runway! Sheer panic and terror convulsed through my body. This was way past the point of aborting the takeoff roll. I was about to ask my plane to do something that even Mr. Piper and his engineers would not demand of the *Spirit of San Diego* on their worst day.

I did not have short field flaps dialed in at 20 degrees because Fred had told me to never do that. Instead I had 10-degree flaps. The plane needed to take off level and flat. Putting it into an unstable configuration at that weight could be a game ender for me. I knew I needed some help from the angels when I spotted the fence coming at me so damn quickly. Seventy knots … 75 knots. That was the last time I saw the speed indicator on that takeoff. My focus shifted to the fence I was rocketing towards.

My plan was to hold the plane on the ground as long as I could, pop it up into the ground effect to clear the fence and then let it settle back down and not stall it. My hope was that when it settled down it would not impact the water. The plane did not initially respond when I first pulled back on the yoke. I was kidding myself. It could not fly at that speed. I would have to play my final hand at the absolute last moment possible so I could accumulate the most speed possible. After what seemed like an eternity I could feel the nose wheel and then the landing gear mains break free of their earthly bounds. As I neared the fence, millimeters and milliseconds became the standard for measurement as opposed to feet and minutes, the *Spirit of San Diego* never questioning what I was requesting of her. She had blind faith that I must know what was best for her … after all I had gotten her this far. From my point of view, I was abusing her terribly like a parent who smacks their child in a fit of rage or panic just a little too hard and can feel the sting on his own hand.

At this point, I felt like I was face to face with the Almighty. The decision was whether I would be taken at this point or allowed to remain on the planet. Had I learned what I was sent to learn or would this trip continue? Time stopped for me and I was bouncing back and forth into the real world and out again.

In a strange way, I was okay with whatever would happen. I thought about the blessed life I had lived, all that I had accomplished and the fact that the people in my life knew I loved them. I knew too that I would be delivered into God's loving hands if I impacted that fence and the water at close to 80 knots in this plane loaded with 4,300 pounds of high-octane aviation fuel and hot metal.

This trip had been hard and I was tired and scared. It would be quick and at least it would finally be over. *No goodbyes*, I thought. Once again, the words of the pilot in Narsarsuaq, Greenland came back to me: "If it starts to get ugly and it is questionable whether you are going to make it, never give up." *Never give up* … my concentration returned to the plane in that instant. I was balancing the climb and airspeed with the tips of my fingers with the absolute lightest touch possible as I cleared the fence. The gods had granted me one more chance at life. This cosmic game was on.

Zen Moment

I was okay with whatever would happen. I thought about the blessed life I had lived, all that I had accomplished and the fact that the people in my life knew I loved them. I knew too that I would be delivered into God's loving hands if I impacted the fence and the water and the worst came to pass...

Chapter 19

Panic Attacks

Following my engine out over Malaysia, I had started waking in the middle of the night with severe panic attacks. I found myself sweating, scared, and unable to sleep, reliving my experiences in graphic detail. As the attack ebbed, I was left feeling shaken, betrayed and questioning my purpose and safety. I had learned in my spiritual psychology class to check in with my inner child about this. I got a very strong response, one I didn't expect this time. This was the same Bobby who first experienced flight with his Dad at age six. He said, *"This isn't fun anymore! I'm scared and I want to go home!"* He was crying hard and extremely clear about how he was feeling. I had never seen my inner child react in this way to anything and I had no idea about how to respond.

All I could say was in the gentlest voice I was capable of: "I'm scared too. I'm unsure of what is ahead for us, but I feel we are being guided. This is bigger than us, and I feel like we need to surrender to what is happening and continue on our journey. It may be the greatest test of our faith, and if it is our time then it is our time."

I don't believe what I said made anything any better with respect to fear and panic attacks, but it was at least the truth that I was sharing. I wasn't going to lie to myself or my inner child. I stood a better chance of surviving the trip if I could deal with the reality I was facing not something that I had dreamed up to ease my fear.

It was obvious to me at this point that there was no way to bail on the trip short of flying the plane home. I had spoken with Mike Borden who is one of the most knowledgeable people I know on the Malibu Mirage at High Performance Aircraft who had bought and sold over one thousand aircraft. He told me in no uncertain terms that my plane could not be shipped home in a shipping container without doing enormous damage to it. The one-piece wing was forty-three feet long and a shipping container is forty feet. To make things even worse the wing was riveted to the plane and separating it would cause damage and be very difficult.

To add insult to injury, I was on Christmas Island, which is the size of a postage stamp in the middle of the Pacific Ocean and over a thousand nautical miles from Hawaii. The prospects didn't look good. And I was scared to death with the longest leg of my trip ahead of me. I was going to have to suck it up and power through this.

After I shared this story with some other pilots I got the response I had expected: "What is your life worth to you? Leave the plane and go home." Well the plane was worth about $400,000 to $500,000 and many people were following my journey, well into the hundreds of thousands. I didn't want to let anyone down. More importantly I felt I was in alignment with my purpose, passion and Spirit, which is the definition of *Flying Thru Life*, the title of my first book. Whatever happened, I knew the story would be amazing and Spirit was providing me with some profound material for my speaking and writing that would follow the trip. This trip would be the vehicle for a powerful and important message for aviation.

I never told anyone I was afraid, but the truth was that after the engine out in Malaysia I was genuinely terrified every day. It was like I was stepping into a flying coffin. I needed to tell someone and felt like I would burst apart if I didn't. I was busy playing the role of the person who inspires, who fights through his fear and goes after his dreams. But I wasn't sure I was taking care of myself—self nurturing.

Eddie from GASE did know what I was going through. Many of his clients flew much smaller, lower flying, riskier and less capable planes on trips like this. I knew he was operating from a place of knowledge and guiding me, but he never pressed me in one direction or the other. He had shared a story of two guys doing a shorter trip in gyrocopters. One had crashed and died and the other one stopped the trip and sent his copter home in a crate. I believe this was his way of telling me it was okay if I decided to do that. The trip had proven so much already. I didn't need to continue. I was comforted knowing Eddie had my back and would do anything to help out. But I also didn't want to appear afraid although I'm sure I did at times. Eddie knew the game and by the end of the trip had become a friend, sponsor and supporter of mine.

To ease my fears, I decided to have conversations with God. I would take out a blank piece of white paper or whatever I could find in my hotel room and write whenever I felt overwhelmed. I wrote directly to God. It looked like this:

Bobby: I'm so fucking scared I don't know that I can go on. Every time I step into that plane, I am afraid for my life and can barely breathe. I just want to get on a commercial plane and go home.

The response I would get was always loving and supportive. The answers were always something like this:

God: Breathe, just breathe.

Bobby: I'm trying.

God: You have been preparing for this your entire life. You are strong. You can do this. You can complete this trip and inspire others to go after their dreams as well.

Bobby: I know all this is happening for my highest good, but it seems so fucking difficult. I'm getting resistance at every point. I feel like I'm at my breaking point.

God: You are given only what you can handle.

Bobby: (Eyes watering) I know what you are telling me is true. But it is so hard to do this day after day.

God: You must surrender completely.

Bobby: I have accepted my death. If this happens, I accept it. I have lived a full life and my faith is strong. But why must I be put through so much?

God: You are being prepared for something greater than you can even imagine.

Bobby: (crying) Somehow I know that. I will continue. I have faith.

God: You are loved more than you will ever know. You are always with me.

Bobby: I know that. Thank you.

I had many conversations like this during the course of the trip. I could always get answers when I needed them even in the late hours of the night. I was comforted in some ways by reaching out directly to God; it strengthened my faith. I knew my mission had a purpose. I was being guided and protected. Surrendering to the will of something other than me was difficult and I had much to learn.

Zen Moment

All I could say was in the gentlest voice I was capable of: "I'm scared too. I'm unsure of what is ahead for us, but I feel we are being guided. This is bigger than us, and I feel like we need to surrender to what is happening and continue on our journey. It may be the greatest test of our faith, and if it is our time then it is our time."

Chapter 20

The Longest and Final Leg

Somewhere over the vast Pacific Ocean at 21,000-23,000 feet on my last open ocean leg. With land nowhere in sight, taking in the beauty of the planet just as the sun begins to set knowing that I still had one final test ahead of me.

The longest and most challenging leg of my trip was the final one from Honolulu, Hawaii, to Monterey, California. Per my Jeppesen navigation software, it was a distance of 2,150 miles. FlightAware would show the distance that I would cover on that leg at over 2,400 miles. That was an immense distance to ask of any aircraft especially a single-engine Piper Malibu Mirage. For me, that seemed an impossibly long distance for man or machine. I knew it would take me over twelve hours and that would be my greatest distance ever flown, longest flight and greatest time and distance over water. The engine would be called to do something I had never asked of her before, to run nonstop for twelve-and-a-half hours. At 2,400 revolutions per minute in an hour it would turn 144,000 times. During the flight the engine and many of its parts would make 1.8 million revolutions.

In some ways, it was interesting that the last leg would be the longest and hardest of the trip. By that time I would be at the top of my flying game but also the most fatigued from the trip. I had exactly three months and seven days to think about this final leg. When I completed a leg, the script was, yes, I completed this leg but I still have the most difficult one to go. The suspense would continue to the point where I could barely stand it.

The final leg had six major stressors that were of great concern to me.

First, I would have to decide the timing of this flight. Since I would be flying from west to east making my days shorter I would have to decide if I wanted to take off in the dark or land in the dark. I spent countless hours thinking about this. The Sulemans had chosen to take off in the darkness when they were fresh but heavy, very heavy. They had the added weight of the second person but a much thicker wing that created more lift than my plane. They were also flying slower and lower than I was so they may have ended up with darkness on both sides. I would have liked to talk to them.

Ultimately I was trying to minimize the time I would be over the water in total darkness. If I had to ditch I didn't want to do it at night. It would be difficult if not impossible to judge the direction of the swells at night and set the aircraft down. Furthermore, determining my orientation in the plane (upside down or right side up) once I impacted the water in the pitch black Pacific would be even more difficult especially if I had been initially knocked out.

I had completed an open-ocean survival class at Corporate Air Parts in Los Angeles just days before I left on the circumnavigation. As part of it we had a segment in which we swam in a pool with our life jackets on and were required to get into a life raft. The raft was so tightly packed with people that we were stacked up on one another with barely enough room to breathe. I heard one of the experienced flight attendants let out a primal scream as someone stepped on her leg. You could feel a wave of panic sweep through the group. The fear was so thick you could cut it with a survival knife. The raft was impossibly tight and the number of people that the raft was certified to carry was absolutely insane. I thought this would be impossible in the open ocean, at night, with injuries, disoriented people, and sharks. This experience made my fear of ditching even more real.

Next, I was concerned about how I would hold up after flying for twelve-plus hours. Flying open ocean legs is fatiguing in itself and characterized by lots of adrenaline. I wondered what the cumulative effects of adrenaline would be on me. I had no way of knowing and I wasn't a college kid who was used to pulling all-nighters before an exam. I was the guy who went to bed each and every night at 11:00 p.m. and woke at 7:00ish the next morning. I would be carrying food with me that would help me peak just before I landed, including fruit, beef jerky, crackers, a sandwich, Garden of Life protein bars and ideally some chocolate with sugar and caffeine.

The fourth and greatest stressor was that I was still unsure of my engine. The loss of engine oil over the Strait of Malacca haunted me on every flight. What was truly the damage that my engine had suffered? Was there some critical component that had been weakened and would fail in flight? I had lingering issues of low manifold pressure and high oil consumption. Oil consumption is not an issue that ever gets better by itself. And how could the mechanic not find the source of the low manifold pressure? He had made adjustments under the guidance of my mechanic back in San Diego, but we were still two inches low on takeoff. I would need all that power to lift off at 27 percent over max gross weight.

The engine was burning about a quart of oil every hour, which told me that that engine was tired and loose and ready for replacement or overhaul. The engine had 1,800 hours on it and was about two hundred hours from the "Time Between Overhaul" (TBO). It was not unusual to run an engine slightly beyond this point by one hundred hours but not recommended beyond that.

Theories abounded about the cause of the oil leak. One was that I was climbing at such a steep and slow rate of 110 knots that the oil was frothing and in turn being blown out the air oil separator.

Another was that the compression and oil rings were lining up and the oil was being blown between where the two sides came together. And finally, since the plane was a little tail heavy, the oil was mostly towards the back of the engine and thus registered a bit lower on the dipstick, which was towards the front of the engine.

In the back of my mind, I wondered if one or both of my turbo chargers were leaking oil and somehow the mechanics had missed it. Later I would be advised to have both sent out and checked by the manufacturer who was better equipped and could determine without a doubt the source of the problem. Either way, I was hyper sensitive after the loss of oil I had experienced over Malaysia. I had Kel Anderson, a fantastic mechanic based in Honolulu, spend an enormous amount of time looking for the problem. I wouldn't leave Hawaii until he had checked everything and had run out of options, even after talking to my mechanic back home.

Deep down I doubted all of the mechanics and my intuition was telling me that everything was not okay. I trusted my intuition and felt this would be an odd time to go against it. My intuition was my direct link to Spirit and with all the inexplicable things that had happened on this trip, I was starting to realize that I had been guided since the very beginning. From all the things that had fallen into place to allow me to take this trip, to my unexplainable luck over the Strait of Malacca, to the impossible takeoff and landings into American Samoa, to the fact that my turbo chargers survived without any oil for a brief time. I could no longer explain my good fortune in surviving all of this except by saying that I was being guided and protected by something bigger than me. Fifth, I was flying the plane at 27 percent over max gross weight. That was higher than the manufacturer had recommended and nobody knew exactly how the plane would fly at that weight. This information wasn't published anywhere and nobody wanted to go out on a limb and give information that could send you to your death. Flying over max gross was one thing that everyone was warned about as beginning pilots and we all had read countless accident reports that attributed the cause of crashes to overloaded planes.

I was so afraid of flying overweight that I had a vision I would fall from the air in a death spiral if I were even slightly over gross. Perhaps this was not scary for a trained ferry pilot with experience, but for someone doing it for the first time, by himself, well, let's just say I was not looking forward to it. In fact, the thought of not lifting off the runway and slamming into a fence or wall at 100 mph with 315 gallons of high-octane aviation fuel was absolutely terrifying.

And finally, there was the issue of using the Turtle Pac rubber fuel tank. I had heard numerous times they were unreliable and required the pilot to get up and move the tank around to get proper fuel flow. For that reason, I had chosen my fifth fuel tank to be metal. I was surprised to find that the sixth solid fuel tank would not fit in my plane and we would be using a thirty-seven-gallon Turtle Pac instead.

This rubber bladder was from the plane of a congressman who had planned to do the same flight but backed down at the last minute, allegedly due to a delay that blew his schedule. I wondered if he just got cold feet at the last minute. Many would say they would do the trip but four out of five yielded to the voices of self-doubt. It was well documented.

I thought back to an early conversation I had had with Dave Hirschman, from AOPA about a trip he had planned to Greenland with a couple of other planes. One of the pilots turned back in Canada at the absolute last minute. He lost his nerve and went home. I couldn't imagine living the rest of my life knowing I had come this far only to back away before the most epic leg of the trip.

I was all in and I knew that. I would surely judge myself a coward to not finish this trip. I had drunk the Kool-Aid but was unsure what was driving me. Was it truly faith or a toxic combination of fear of failure and ego? How could I tell the difference? I kept asking myself, how would this end?

What a cruel turn it would be for the Universe to allow me to make it this far but then take me on my final leg after nearly twenty-four thousand miles and twenty-two countries. Surely that would be unacceptable even to the gods if this was all just for their entertainment? Weren't they compassionate? Perhaps they had seen this countless times and were just looking for more dramatic ways for the story to end.

I thought back to my three years of graduate-level spiritual psychology training. I could not believe that the voices in my head could be true this time. I knew that the Universe wanted the best for me. I believed that all that was happening was for my highest good. What I was feeling did not feel loving like intuition but instead felt like fear in its rawest form. The ugly and desperate face of fear once again popped its head up, along for the ride. He was the copilot I couldn't see that night over American Samoa. I realized at this moment he wasn't bad or evil; he was just struggling to stay alive in the most dreadful of circumstances like me. I needed to silence my mind and get back to my task at hand: survival.

Needless to say, my mind was very busy on that last and unbelievably long leg. I remember approaching the plane on the tarmac at sunrise on a quiet Honolulu morning before anyone was around and asking the *Spirit of San Diego* to get me home safely. I thanked her for her heroic performance on this journey around the world. I realized I had been along for the ride and she was the one making all this happen in the physical world.

I wondered if we could truly love a machine. All the pistons, push rods, valves, bolts and metal structures. It was like someone had breathed life into her like the Tin Man in *The Wizard of Oz*. "Did she have a soul?" was what I wondered more than anything. To me she was more than the sum of her components. She was heart, soul, spirit, dreams, power, energy and, to me, love all wrapped up into the coolest toy in the world. A toy so grand and amazing that I could climb inside and become a part of her. A toy that made me feel like Superman. Clearly by this time we had become one.

I ultimately decided that my best chance for survival was to take off at sunrise where I could see the visual horizon and mountains in front of me. I would be the most alert in the morning and able to handle the plane, which was heavily loaded with fuel and the most challenging to fly. In the back of my mind the consequence of this decision was playing out like a kid's stereo at full blast: "nighttime landing into a non-towered airport, with mountains after flying for 12-plus hours."

I requested Runway Right (8R) out of Honolulu, which gave me twelve thousand feet of runway to get the plane into the air. I would have a turn to the right to avoid the mountains in the distance. Compounding the stress from the early morning departure and the enormous weight of my plane with 317 gallons of aviation fuel was the fact that my plane was making only forty-one inches of manifold pressure. Forty-two inches was redline and forty-three was what my mechanic said was ideal for takeoff. In cruise, I needed only twenty-nine inches but getting into the air was an entirely different story.

I wished I had the extra two inches of manifold pressure when I would be flying heavier than ever. My mechanic in Hawaii was great, but even working over the phone with my mechanic in San Diego could not get the full manifold pressure we wanted. An adjustment had been made to the engine to get the manifold pressure up, but it wasn't the source of the problem. It was like turning up the volume on a sound system when you couldn't hear the music because you had cotton balls in your ears. No one mechanic can be an expert on all planes but he was the best I was going to get short of flying someone over to Hawaii to work on the plane and thus delaying my trip even further.

I taxied to the runway from the repair station, wanting to get in the air as soon as possible. Each second I waited equated to another second I would have to fly in total darkness over the Pacific Ocean.

My palms were sweaty and I could feel my heart pounding hard in my chest. I thought, *I don't need to do this more than once in my life.* The *Spirit of San Diego* looked like a low rider with the tail closer to the ground than usual and the tires bulging out. I wondered if perhaps I should have put more air in the tires with this enormous weight in fuel I was carrying. I called ground control and was given my flight route and taxi instructions. I did my run up and then I was given clearance. "November Niner Niner Seven Mike Alpha cleared for takeoff Runway 8 Right." I had also been given an enormously complicated departure procedure that I had flown a couple days before while test flying the plane.

I positioned the plane at the absolute end of the runway to get the longest roll possible. I slowly ran the engine up to full power, which was forty-two inches in this case, versus the forty-three I was used to. The throttle control had become sensitive and would fluctuate wildly if I made adjustments too fast. This was it, the moment of truth. The impossibly long leg of my trip, the one I dreaded for the last three months and seven days, was here. None of what I had accomplished on the previous legs would matter if I blew this leg. The months of detailed planning, repairs, sponsorship calls, social media, book preparations and blogging would be wiped away.

I was rolling the dice yet another time on this trip. Would the turbochargers hold? Would my engine run out of oil? Would I get caught up in the brutal weather of the Intertropical Convergence Zone? Would my plane even fly in this configuration? Would my seventeen-year old aircraft fail me? Would I ever see another soul? Would I be taken?

I had no idea that I would be afraid for my life for the entire last third of the trip.

Zen Moment

Though the mechanics were telling me otherwise, my intuition was telling me that everything was not okay. I trusted my intuition and found this an odd time to go against it. My intuition was my direct link to Spirit and with all the inexplicable things that had happened on this trip, I was starting to realize that I had been guided since the very beginning.

Zen Moment

The ugly and desperate face of fear once again popped its head up, along for the ride. He was the copilot I couldn't see that night over American Samoa. I realized at this moment he wasn't bad or evil; he was just struggling to stay alive in the most dreadful of circumstances like me. I needed to silence my mind and get back to my task at hand: survival.

Chapter 21

Coming Home

This journey would take me to places I had never been before on the planet and in my personal and spiritual development. I questioned everything: my motives, my ability, my mechanics, and the Universe. This trip would be a test of my strength and, at times, turn out to be more like a fight for survival. I would be asking the Universe if I had fulfilled my purpose here on the planet and if I would be taken before my return to the United States. Was my purpose in fact to share what I was experiencing or was this just going to be a journey that ended with a fizzle, bang or an explosive thud?

I said a quick prayer hoping to calm myself:

I look skyward and open my heart and soul to the connection that is always available to me.

I express gratitude for my living, healthy and light-filled body. It is home to my soul and the means by which I am able to fly my wondrous plane.

I am grateful for this living, thriving and beautiful planet that I explore as I soar effortlessly through the heavens.

I am thankful for my amazing flying machine that lifts me into the heavens as I float on oceans of billowing white clouds.

I am blessed for all those who share the magical experience of flight with me. I ask for their health.

As my soul reconnects with the earth, I accept the lessons I have been given on my flight and surrender for my highest good!

I let the brakes go without giving another instant of time to my old nasty friend "self-doubt." I had heard enough from him. I was rolling and the 350-hp twin-turbocharged Lycoming engine was thundering! I could feel my heart pounding almost out of my chest "*Boom* Boom, *Boom* Boom." One leg left, one leg … I thought for a second what a fiery and smoky mess this plane would make at the end of the runway if I couldn't get airborne. My speed was increasing and I could see I had a lot of runway ahead of me. My normal rotation speed was 85 knots at 10 degrees of flaps and I was waiting until 100 knots because I was this impossibly heavy.

At 95 knots the plane was bouncing a bit like she wanted up and at 100 knots I was flying. I was lighter than air at that point and had used about three-quarters of the runway. I was off on the longest leg of my life. My soul was once again "Flying Thru Life" as it always was meant to. I was answering my childhood calling. It had taken me over forty years since my first dream of flight to answer this incessant calling. But it was happening. I was in the hands of God being lifted up by all those that were supporting me. This was what it meant to fly.

I was praying, almost begging, for a drama-free 2,150 nautical miles, but I knew once more that I had obstacles to overcome and lessons to learn. This was far from over and what was happening was scripted for my highest good. I realized there would be no fiery crash at the end of the runway. I would not be taken there. I was relieved and could see nothing but blue sky and clouds ahead of me. This was the real deal I thought. This was not a casual adventure that people luck their way through. It was a dream unfolding right in front of me.

The plane climbed reasonably well once it was in the air despite its heavy load of fuel. I was thankful for all the time I had spent reducing the weight of the plane. I had twenty-four quarts of oil with me, which was an indication of my absolute and total paranoia with respect to the oil burn on this trip. I wasn't going to let this plane run out of oil or if it did I was going to buy myself the time I needed to prepare for a ditching in the vast Pacific Ocean.

I would climb to thirteen thousand feet, burn off the fuel in the Turtle-Pac first to eliminate that risk then it was on to my tried-and-true 140-gallon metal tank, which doubled as an explosion simulator. I shifted tanks with about two gallons in the Turtle-Pac, which I had calculated based on my fuel burn and quite simply it looked like it had about two gallons left in it. I was relieved to be done with that tank forever. The tank itself had more warnings than a pack of cigarettes. I was told not to put my full weight on the Turtle-Pac while climbing over but I knew that was impossible with all the gear around it. The best I could do was to place my weight on the edges of it so that my weight would collapse the outside edge of the Turtle-Pac and be supported by a flattened outer piece and not increase the pressure on the seams. The problem was when the tank was full it looked like a stuffed pig that was ready to explode, and it was impossible to just put your weight on the seams. I questioned whether I was doing damage to it as I passed over. At this point, it really didn't matter anymore. That was a problem for the next guy who would use the tank, not me.

The metal tank had no warnings on it and was just six pieces of shiny aluminum welded together in a rectangular shape. Perhaps they assumed if you were using it you had a death wish so marking it up with warnings was just a waste of time anyway.

I was cruising at thirteen thousand feet because the plane did not want to fly higher in that heavy configuration. I flew at this altitude gradually climbing higher as I got lighter. I had my face glued to the instruments wondering how the *Spirit of San Diego* could be managing all this stress. It felt like my heart was skipping every other beat.

Once I had burned another fifty gallons off the metal tank, I was back to the same 10 percent over gross configuration that I knew so well from other parts of the trip. Now it was time to go up to my happy place of twenty-one thousand feet in elevation where I felt the most comfortable. The plane liked this altitude and as it got lighter and lighter it also got faster and faster, not to mention easier to fly and more stable. I was getting close to the cruise speed of 195 knots that I knew the plane was cable of doing. I was looking around and in good spirits. I had a solid night's sleep and felt I had the reserves to do this twelve- to fourteen-hour flight. The winds were as forecast and I had a ten-knot push from behind for the first two-thirds of the trip.

I was getting closer to California with each passing minute and watching the GPS count off nautical miles one at a time. I remember passing one thousand nautical miles thinking I still had a long way to go. *Who does this?* I thought. I looked out as far as I could see and nothing but big white billowing clouds and blue, blue, blue. I started to daydream and thought to myself that it was inconceivable how much water is really on this planet. I knew somebody had probably already calculated just how much we were talking about and it was more than I could get my mind around. I still hadn't been able to get my mind around what I was doing. It was just one more leg. The word "epic" came to mind.

I had been instructed to turn the HF radio on once I was about seventy-five miles out from Honolulu. I was reporting my position every hour. The radio was constantly hissing, popping and shrieking. I could hear the commercial airline pilots reporting their positions as well. I thought about the fact that they were doing this trip with much less stress than I was. No HF radio power supply and heat source mounted one-quarter inch from a fuel tank sitting behind them; no piston engine pounding away at 2,400 rpm trying to blow itself apart; no issues of low manifold pressure; no mystery oil-loss issue but instead two or four giant Rolls-Royce turbofan engines that were each purring away one hundred times more reliably than mine. They had multiple pilots so one could take a nap if he got tired and let's not forget lots of hot food and flight attendants.

I thought, *I need a flight attendant.* On my next trip I would definitely have one. Need to use the restroom on a commercial plane? No problem it's right behind the cockpit. The larger commercial planes also had the advantages of altitude and speed. The higher altitudes of thirty- to thirty-nine thousand feet would give them a greater gliding distance and the weather was often smoother and clear of clouds as compared to me down low at twenty-one thousand feet. They were flying at slightly more than double my speed, which meant their trip was five to six hours, not twelve and a half.

I was adding a quart of oil to the engine every one to two hours even though the mechanic was convinced the plane was not burning it. I thought I would just blow out any excess and make a mess on the bottom of the plane.

I was flying along thinking, I have this made! The enormous stress I had been feeling for the last three months and a week was nearly over! It had been one hell of a trip, and soon I would be back in my comfortable bed in San Diego trying to put all these pieces together. I had only blue skies ahead. This was clearly going to be a great victory and when I zoomed out on my GPS I could see the mainland of California. Even saying the name

California brought me comfort after being to so many unusual and wondrous places I had never heard of before like Kiribati and Noumea, New Caledonia.

I was six hundred nautical miles off the coast of California and feeling pretty relaxed. The *Spirit of San Diego* was cruising along and the engine was creating the deepest, most beautiful growl. I was listening to one of my favorite songs via Bluetooth. Life could not be better. My passion was in total alignment with my purpose and I felt that I was "Flying Thru Life."

My real life was as good as anything I had ever dreamed. For an instant in time the two were one. I realized I had created the reality of this moment through the dreams of my lifetime. This was no coincidence! This moment had been carefully orchestrated one step at a time in every detail from my childhood starting with my first interest in planes. I've been here doing what I was always intended to do. I'd melded my dreams and reality and have become the voice for something bigger than I thought possible.

As I recognized the dream, my first thought was that I needed to stay with the plane and this was not the time to drift off. I forced myself to take the hourly engine readings as I had for the last 147 hours before. First I noted the time, which was approximately sixty minutes from the last reading. Outside air temperature -12 degrees Celsius, cylinder head temperature 375 degrees Fahrenheit, oil pressure 63 psi check, oil temperature 200 Fahrenheit ... *OMG* I'm overheating! This was no dream; this was a nightmare.

The engine was undergoing extreme heat stress and would be screaming in agony if it could speak. In my mind's eye I could see the engine steaming and smoking oil turning black from the red-hot metal. My reading was 200 degrees Fahrenheit and I felt my heart skip a beat. I was all adrenaline. My engine was *definitely* overheating! The oil temperature had been 190 to 193 for the entire trip, including throughout North Africa and the Middle East, where temperatures had reached 114 degrees Fahrenheit on the ground.

I was right all along about that oil leak. Damn those mechanics! I had been trailing oil for 1,500 nautical miles across the Pacific. Immediately I pumped three quarts of oil into the engine. *No change!* I was afraid and I felt panic pulse through my body once again. I said to myself, "Oh God not now, I'm so close!" I throttled back two inches of manifold pressure and patiently waited … *still no change!*

My heart was pounding hard. I was still too far away from the coast of California to bumble my way in with a poorly functioning plane. Could fate really be this cruel? I throttled back to twenty-five and eventually to twenty-three inches of manifold pressure. This was barely enough to keep the plane in the air and as the plane slowed, the angle of attack of the plane started to increase. The nose was rising and the airspeed was dropping. With less airflow over the wings, the plane needed its nose up more in order to fly and that was not very efficient.

This was not a good long-term solution; I would need to burn more fuel to stay in the air this way because the plane was creating so much drag. But at least the engine had cooled and I figured I had an extra two to three hours of fuel, which would help flying in this inefficient configuration. Breathing deeply, I kept telling myself to calm down, the engine was still running. I tried a few more combinations of rpm and manifold pressure settings that didn't help the problem.

I started sending satellite text messages on my DeLorme InReach Explorer to different mechanics and knowledgeable people. Mike Borden at High Performance Aircraft responded immediately. He started asking me for different engine temperatures and would in turn give me different engine settings to try. I was still panicked, but at least I knew I had help that I needed *if* there was a solution.

We went back and forth for about thirty minutes and nothing seemed to change the oil temperature. Eventually we determined that I was in an unusually hot pocket of air. At twenty-one thousand feet the outside air temperature was only -11 degrees Celsius. The fact that the engine temperature did not continue to rise was the tipoff that things had stabilized. The final text from Mike said to do nothing and as long as it didn't climb any further we would just leave it alone.

The last few hours were filled with enormous anticipation and stress. I must have looked at that oil temperature gauge a thousand times.

It was about thirty minutes after we had agreed to just keep an eye on the oil temperature that the unthinkable happened. I heard an extremely loud thud come from inside the engine compartment. By this time I had become used to the loud bangs from inside the fuselage caused by the ferry tank. But this sounded like a belt letting go or a mechanical component breaking apart. It was sudden and it took my breath away. I watched in terror once again waiting for the instruments to reveal what had happened at twenty-one thousand feet and now about five hundred nautical miles out.

I stared at the panel, checking and rechecking my engine readings. It was torture, like being a trapped bird in a cage that someone kept banging on for his or her entertainment.

My heart was nearly pounding out of my chest and I was angry! All I could think was how cruel this was all becoming. I shouted out loud, "If you are going to f'ing take me let's get this over with and don't put me through all this." What could I possibly need to learn from all this? What a leg this was turning out to be.

It took me about thirty minutes to calm down and I would never find out what that thud really was. We never found any defective parts, any damage to the plane or came up with any reasonable explanation. I remember watching the sun set and trying to calm myself further. It was going to be another dreaded night landing for me. Once again the 1 percent of aviation that I didn't feel like I had a tight grip on… night landing, overcast weather, uncontrolled airport, mountains and to add insult to injury, I was now exhausted from so much stress!

Finally after what seemed an eternity, I could start to see Monterey on the normal range setting on my Garmin GTN750 GPS. I was three hundred nautical miles out, then two hundred nautical miles, finally one hundred nautical miles and, at last, it was time for descent. I asked to stay at twenty-one thousand feet as long as possible so that if necessary it would be possible for me to coast into this airport surrounded with mountains at night. I remember thinking that would really suck....

My body had been pumping nonstop adrenaline for the several hours and now it was time to put the *Spirit of San Diego* down on terra firma. This landing would require all the concentration, all the calm, all the energy, all the Zen I could muster. I realized that the Universe would not give up this victory without taking me to my absolute limits and then beyond. I honestly didn't think I had much more to give.

My satellite weather was finally working for the first time in three months. The coverage was very limited worldwide and usually about fifteen to thirty minutes late, an eternity in weather time. And as luck would have it, the picture wasn't very good. Solid overcast about two thousand feet over the runway. The air traffic controller confirmed it. His plan was to bring me in low at three thousand feet and if I could see the airport I could land under visual conditions. If not, I would be required to climb to five thousand feet and do a formal instrument approach into Monterey.

I love Monterey. My family owned property there at one time and it was a great place to go on a weekend. I thought back to my last instrument approach there when my iPad software did not georeference my plane onto the approach chart. It was a surprise and made the landing more difficult. I wondered if the iPad software would work this time. I had thoughts that if it was all going to end, at least Monterey was a place that I enjoyed, they would find what was left of my body, and it would be close to where everyone lived. I caught myself and attempted to remove these thoughts from my mind. "Cancel, cancel," I said repeatedly.

As I got within two miles of the Monterey airport I could see absolutely nothing but a sea of clouds. They seemed to be lit up from below and that was it, no distinguishable landmarks. Now faced with a sea of clouds over coastal mountains I was dared to take one last chance.

In hindsight, I should have passed on the instrument landing and gone further inland to Salinas, but I didn't see walking away from a challenge like this on the final leg. It felt like wimping out at the last possible moment or walking away from the bully when he is calling you names in front of the pretty girls. Common sense tells you to walk away but your honor says to punch him right in the face. Perhaps it was bravado, stupidity, "Get-There-Itis," but I was going to give this a try. My plane had become part of me by this time or perhaps me part of it. We were one and she had stuck with me through one hell of a trip. I was going to do this right.

I called the air traffic controller back and reported that I could not see the airport. He gave me instructions to climb to five thousand feet to clear the mountains and to await vectors to the initial approach fix for the instrument approach. I complied and watched the red splotches on my GPS begin to turn yellow as I climbed to avoid terrain. The red represented mountaintops and extreme danger to me. The air traffic controller came back on and gave me a few turns and instructed me, "November Niner Niner Seven Mike Alpha proceed to the Salinas IAF (initial approach fix)." I clicked five times on the communications or "comm" button on my yoke to turn on the pilot-controlled lighting at the airport. I couldn't remember if it was five or seven. I asked the air traffic controller and after a few minutes he came back with an "I don't know … perhaps try both." Five clicks seemed right to me, but I clicked it about fifty times just to be sure. I came to the IAP (initial approach point) and lined up on a course of 214 degrees, which would take me directly into the airport where I would be required to make a final right turn to line up on the runway heading of 280 degrees.

I descended into the clouds around four thousand feet and was violently tossed about. I could see the plane's landing lights reflecting off the clouds back into my eyes. Out the window I could see only about five feet in front of me, not an inch more. Descending at almost 200 mph with mountains to my left, I couldn't see a damn thing. I would hand-fly the plane at these difficult times; while some airlines required that autopilots be used, in general aviation the glide slopes don't always couple with the autopilot and then you have bigger problems.

If something went wrong at this critical phase of the flight, I figured I could at least blame it on myself and not the autopilot. And losing an autopilot would force me to hand-fly the plane anyway, so this was me being prepared and not giving the Universe an opportunity to make my situation worse. It was clearly the hardest thing you would ever be called to do in flying except perhaps deal with in-flight emergencies during an instrument approach. At this point, I was expecting anything.

At that moment I thought, *if there is a God or gods they are watching me right now very carefully.* I was unsure if I was entertainment, but I knew I had their attention. I was in control because they had thrown everything they had at me on this leg and now it was up to me to make it happen or slam into the side of the mountain in a fiery ball of metal, fuel and hot oil. I pictured them like a kid with his face too close to the TV watching his favorite show. He may risk going cross-eyed, but it is worth it because the show is so damn good!

A sense of calm came over me just as I broke out of the clouds. The violent thrashing had stopped, I could see the runway lit up before me, the mountains were behind me and to the left. The gear was down and lights on. I dropped the flaps and set the propeller for landing configuration. I was floating on a layer of air, I felt weightless and free like a bird with his wings outstretched waiting for his soul to reconnect with the earth one more time. It was bliss and it was happening in slow motion.

As I felt a slight bump and heard the tires chirp I knew I was on the ground. Once the nose gently touched down I lightly pressed on the brakes and the plane started to slow and I knew I had arrived! I raised my right hand, did a fist pump and yelled, "YES! I DID IT!" Twenty-six thousand miles, twenty-three countries and five continents. As I taxied to the FBO I lined up on a parking space and shut down that big Lycoming engine. I took my first full breath in three months and eight days. I had arrived back in the continental United States.

I shut off the fuel, grabbed my iPad and phone, unbuckled my seatbelt and airbag and started to climb over the Turtle-Pac. I could hear the unused fuel swish and slush in the tank. I realized that all my worry about this fuel tank was unwarranted; it had worked well. Proper installation was important as with any modification to an aircraft.

I could not process all I had been through. It was inconceivable to me. The trip flashed through my mind, something like the way a person's life does as they are dying. I could see it all. Every detail, every moment, every frustration ... I unlatched the clamshell hatch unlocking the top and then the bottom, which entailed pulling out a cable and then supporting the weight of the door with the cable and slowly lowering it. As the door opened and the fresh air rushed into the cabin I could smell the characteristic cool sea air I knew so well from Monterey. As I stepped down the steps after being cramped up in my seat for more than twelve and one-half hours and dealing with some of the most stressful moments of the trip and my life, I planted my feet firmly on the ground. I straightened my back slowly and thought to myself, *OMG, I'm alive, I have made it. Yes!*

Out of the darkness came a young man who greeted me. He was the only guy working at the FBO that night. He smiled at me in the dim light of overcast night. I could see trucks driving down the runway out of the corner of my eye. The first thing he said to me was, "You just made it in before they shut down the runway for construction."

I laughed and said, "Luck and his close friend fear have been with me on this trip. I'm glad the Universe has been looking out for me…" I walked away from the plane turning back to get one last look at my beautiful woman, the *Spirit of San Diego*, and I felt that on this day I had lived completely. My passion and purpose were in alignment with the Universe, I was "Flying Thru Life."

The next morning just before a short hop to Lake Tahoe to visit my Dad, I checked the oil level in the engine: sixteen quarts, which was five more than the maximum. *How is that even possible*, I - inside the engine. That couldn't have been good.

Zen Moment

I realized I had created the reality of this moment through the dreams of my lifetime. This was no coincidence! This moment had been carefully orchestrated one step at a time in every detail from my childhood starting with my first interest in planes.

Zen Moment

This landing would require all the concentration, all the calm, all the energy, all the Zen I could muster. The Universe would not give up this victory without taking me to my absolute limits and then beyond.

Chapter 22

Zen Pilot Version 2.0

My arrival in San Diego was a surreal experience. No longer would I be hearing the constant drone of the high frequency radio just inches behind my head that sounded like someone was calling me from the afterlife. I wouldn't smell the Avgas fumes that had vented overnight from ferry tanks five and six, or worry that they might ignite and explode. I wouldn't be wiping the AeroShell 15W-50 oil off my hand that spilled during my emergency landing into Kuala Lumpur International 2 Airport or trying to move around the cockpit in my neoprene immersion suit that made me look like a big red Gumby toy.

Instead, I was doing my daily walk through beautiful lush and green Balboa Park where

Lindbergh had walked years before and once again I felt as if I was dreaming like I had so many times on my trip. I was again experiencing the beauty, peace and tranquility of the park while adjusting back to my life at home. I am finding truth in Deepak Chopra's quote that sometimes the dream is more real than our reality. Certainly things were familiar, but not as I expected. I was reminded of my experience while in Indonesia when I visited my elementary school, childhood home, and the pool/club where I had played forty years before. I had spent two and a-half years in these places as a child, but I was shocked at how differently things looked to me as an adult.

I suddenly realized that I had changed and was now seeing the world through a different set of eyes. Life can never be the same if we are growing and evolving. As a citizen of the world my boundaries between countries had been removed and I experienced firsthand that all of us wish for joy, happiness, health, freedom, love, peace of mind and to fulfill our most impossibly big dreams no matter where we are from. I was experiencing a new reality.

Part of this was driven by the deep sense of gratitude that I felt because I made it safely around the world after several very close calls. There were times when I doubted myself and my aircraft, and moments of being unsure what the next millisecond held for me. Sometimes I felt that I didn't want to fly or was experiencing a great deal of uncertainty, which would wake me up in the middle of the night as I was shaken by what had happened on earlier parts of the trip. The voices of self-doubt had their audience to sternly express their most unsettling thoughts. My faith was put to the test.

Somehow I persevered. It would have been so easy for the story to end at any point along the way, but that did not happen. I was spared for a purpose bigger than what I knew. My faith had been tested "off the scale." It took enormous trust to get back into an aircraft after some of these events. I ceased to pray for safety, but instead asked for whatever was intended for my highest learning to happen. This was surrender in its purest form. It scared me deeply, but I also knew the biggest learning lesson of my life was unfolding right in front of my eyes.

For the last ninety-eight days I had been focused on what was happening in the moment. It was the only way I could stay safe. My range of view was simply as far as the leg I was attempting to complete. I spent little time thinking about what happened yesterday or what the schedule was for the following day. I was reading gauges, looking out for other aircraft, talking to air traffic controllers, checking and rechecking my course, studying charts, adjusting engine performance, ensuring my emergency devices were ready as well as keeping an eye on the weather.

It seemed that even though the flying portion of this trip was complete, I was still processing and downloading what I was intended to learn. My sense was this would continue for a long time to come. It's been said that life hands us lessons only as fast as we are ready to learn them. Certainly the lessons don't stop when we embark on our journey. If anything, they accelerate and come in divine order to help heal our hurt and help us remain open to love.

I would wake many times in the middle of the night wondering if my trip was real or just another dream. I was anxious and confused. It would take a few minutes but then I would think to myself, of course it was real and if I doubted it I could always go back to the social media and look at the articles and interviews. But is any of that real? Maybe my mind was projecting this reality and I was creating it all. It was an illusion I had created just for me. But one night I decided to have another conversation with God. Let him know that I felt stuck. That I was expecting some other things to come my way ... though what they might be I did not know. God spoke to me clearly and let me know before I could move forward I must first process all the lessons from my trip. Just as in life we can't move ahead until we have learned what we need to go to the next level. This message rang true in the absolute dead silence of the night. These messages came always in the silence, in the privacy of my thoughts. They were always divine and loving.

My business seemed less and less important to me. Other people were handling that for the duration of my trip. The business that thrilled me several months before just seemed like an annoyance now. I seemed to have moved on and was trying to put the pieces of my new life together again. What did all this mean? Would my message be one of inspiration? Overcoming fear? Dreaming impossibly big? Manifesting? Silence? Faith?

I remembered back to the first time I thought about a trip around the world; it seemed beyond possibility, reason and reality. But somehow it was now behind me. Even Lindbergh struggled after his return. There wasn't a place in the world for him. He had done something to change the world but he didn't fit in anymore. Was it better to be anonymous?

People annoyed me. I was in a funk. I didn't feel like hanging out with anyone. I was seeing faults and not the good in them. They wanted to hear the stories, but they were too impatient to hear them all. Long walks in the park would calm me. Honestly I just wanted to hop in my plane again and go. I was seeking out quiet. Everyone asked what next? I hadn't even processed the trip. They were greater adrenaline junkies than I was and had no idea the chances I had taken. I thought, *I had no idea the chances I took.*

I would eventually realize there was my life before my around-the-world trip and my life after it. The circumnavigation represented a defining moment and a turning point for me. I began to think that few things were impossible. Now that I had finally gotten my arms around the world, it was time to embrace everyone and everything. I had global reach and a following that wanted more. More adventure, exploration and the learning that came with it. What started as a trip was just the beginning of something many times bigger. It was an announcement to the world that I had a message and wanted to share it with everyone around the world. Maybe the Universe had intentionally sent me on this trip. Maybe it was a contract that I had when I came into the world. Maybe it was now up to me?

A couple weeks after I returned to the mainland I got down to the business of getting the plane back to its original configuration. That meant another trip to visit my friend Fred Sorenson in Las Vegas and have his crew remove the ferry tanks, auxiliary oil system and HF radio. I spent the day there watching and learning what I could.

I was not prepared for the exchange I would have with Fred. It was one of the most chilling conversations of my life. Fred had a way of turning my world upside down with a single comment. This conversation would be no different than the ones I had before with him including the "How are you alive?" conversation. I told him about the panic attacks I was having after my engine-out in Malaysia, which were especially strong the nights before my five 1,000-to- 2,200-nautical-mile legs over the Pacific. I also shared with him my fears about drowning in the Pacific Ocean and the sense of wanting to simply end the trip, go home and never fly again.

What Fred told me next shocked me. He stopped working on the forward storage compartment where the fuel line from the ferry tanks connected to the engine fuel supply system and looked up as if thinking.

He said, "Each night before an open ocean leg, I vomit and then again the next morning before the flight." He then looked at me as if to remind me that I had been living in a different plane of existence between life and death. To have such a strong physical response, Fred had obviously not made peace with this place in between. I wondered if his life would end over some remote ocean. Really, how does someone who doesn't know how to swim survive five hundred open-ocean crossings? It was only a matter of when. And then as if he was satisfied with his explanation, he went back to work on the forward storage compartment. It was as if he had accepted his fate and there was no sense in fighting it.

That moment I stood there silently, my mouth open as I tried to comprehend what all that meant … why was I alive? And even more so, how in the world was Fred alive? I took a step back and the hangar was quiet. The other guys were equally as bowled over by this comment as I was.

I found what Fred said absolutely frightening and chilling. As I mentioned earlier, he was one of the most accomplished ferry pilots on the planet with over five hundred Pacific crossings and almost 140 in single-engine piston planes. And he was even more terrified than I was. Perhaps I should have been even more concerned.

I had taken enormous risks each and every day of the trip. The people who had begged me not to do the trip were in fact right. I was subjecting myself to risks far beyond what I even knew. If I had successfully made this trip it could only have been with the help of Spirit. It would have been so easy so many times for it to have just been fatally over. I had a purpose beyond the trip, things I needed to share that were important for the rest of the world to know. Things related to flying, pursuing dreams and most importantly, faith, oneness, silence and being guided.

Flying around the world didn't make me a more confident pilot. If anything, it made me more aware of the risks that were possible. I had become more paranoid, detailed, serious, cautious and just simply afraid. I was questioning what I could really control in my life.

Lesson learned, miracles in process

During my trip I realized I was gently being nudged and at other times forcefully moved in a direction of growth. On a daily basis it was sometimes hard to see the progress, direction or how so many pieces could possibly be joined together. But, over time it became clear. And although I always asked that this change happen with "grace and ease" on a daily basis, I'm reminded that growth is not always the easiest process. I was dealing with uncertainty, awkwardness, frustration, anxiety and my very old friend I know so well who goes by the name "self-doubt."

But then I remind myself of all the synchronicities that were happening right in front of me.

The synchronicities are the extra help that I get when I'm in total alignment with my purpose. It's like a bunch of magnets placed randomly on a table. No single one can do much, but when they are in sync the force seems to compound and suddenly there is an order of magnitude that I could not imagine.

For example, when one of my mentors Mary Marcdante suggested I connect with local kids if we are to inspire the next generation of youth to fly, and then discovering that there was a school named after Charles Lindbergh just miles from my home airport. On my first attempt to connect with the Lindbergh Schweitzer Elementary school I got a call one hour later from another mentor who knows the principal Victoria Peterson. I then wrote an email to the principal who is managing two schools at once with a new staff, yet took the time to immediately write back the next day. Perhaps something was unfolding in front of me for my highest and best good?

Another example was when I wondered how in the world I would pay for a trip this big and expensive, and the family of someone I lent money to ten years earlier decided to repay the debt even though their son who took out the loan is now deceased. Or that investors came forward wanting to refinance loans at lower interest rates, or that a promise from childhood to pay for a piece of my advanced graduate degree in spiritual psychology materialized after years of being ignored. In all, I had eleven financial windfalls in two months. I wouldn't think much of one. Two I would call lucky, three I would start to look for another explanation—but eleven!? I needed to look for another explanation. How is that even possible? And that doesn't even include my thirty-seven sponsors who stood behind me with the strength of their businesses, experience, their faith, and their dreams that I carry with me.

And I'm reminded that I don't need to figure all the details out on my own. I've got new and old friends around me encouraging me along every step of the way, helping me and looking out for my interests. Contributing to my efforts with their ideas, experience and wisdom. In a way my friends were carrying me on my dream when the load was too heavy for me alone. I am reminded that we are never truly alone.

The strange thing is that when I am traveling this much I don't feel that any one place is really home. In fact, my home seems to be every country I'm visiting. My world is expanding and as I change this reality it seems clear that the entire planet is where I belong. I am a citizen of the world. I'm seeing more similarities than differences between people and places. My particular hometown, religion, color, and ethnicity are not as important as my desire for joy, happiness, health, freedom, adventure and peace. These are the things that connect me to all the wonderful people I have met and who have treated me like family.

I'm realizing that when I'm in total alignment with my passion, purpose and Spirit, anything is possible and I am in fact "Flying Thru Life." More importantly, I've come to believe that all this is possible not just for me, but also for you and for everyone on the planet.

We are all citizens of the world. Let's keep "Flying Thru Life" together!

Robert DeLaurentis, Zen Pilot

Zen Moment

I ceased to pray for safety, but instead asked for whatever was intended for my highest learning to happen. This was surrender in its purest form. It scared me deeply, but I also knew the biggest learning lesson of my life was unfolding right in front of my eyes.

Zen Moment

That I had successfully made this trip could only have been with the help of Spirit. I had a purpose beyond the trip. There were things I needed to share that were important for the rest of the world to know. Things related to flying, pursuing dreams and most importantly, faith, oneness, silence and being guided.

Zen Moment

It's been said that life hands us lessons only as fast as we are ready to learn them. Certainly the lessons don't stop when we embark on our journey. If anything, they accelerate and come in divine order to help heal our hurt and help us remain open to love.

Zen Moment

During my trip I realized I was gently being nudged and at other times forcefully moved in a direction of growth. On a daily basis it was sometimes hard to see the progress, direction or how so many pieces could possibly be joined together. But, over time it became clear.

Zen Moment

The synchronicities are the extra help that I get when I'm in total alignment with my purpose. It's like a bunch of magnets placed randomly on a table. No single one can do much, but when they are in sync the force seems to compound and suddenly there is an order of magnitude that I could not imagine.

Zen Moment

I ceased to pray for safety, but instead asked for whatever was intended for my highest learning to happen. This was surrender in its purest form. It scared me deeply, but I also knew the biggest learning lesson of my life was unfolding right in front of my eyes.

Bonus Chapter

As a special bonus to my readers of *Zen Pilot* I'm making available an incredible story about my miraculous landing at Samedan Airport just outside of St. Moritz, Switzerland in my Piper Malibu Mirage during my 2013 European trip.

You don't want to miss reading it!

Sign up here for your immediate download
and join me on another
Zen Pilot adventure Flying Thru Life:
http://bit.ly/bonus-chapter

Here's a short excerpt:

Angel of Death Over Samedan

"At the instant I heard her say those words, the stall warning horn went off and I could feel the plane instantly and helplessly dropping. At forty feet off the ground I slammed the throttle forward to full as fast as I could, which was terrible for the engine, the landing gear, and me, but I had no option. *If I survive this impact,* I thought, *I'm going to be stuck in the Swiss Alps for weeks.* The landing gear is the weakest point on a Malibu Mirage and I was almost certain I was about to pancake all three of them and myself against the rock hard Swiss Alps."

Sign up here for your immediate download:
http://bit.ly/bonus-chapter

Appendix One

Spirit of San Diego Innovations

Altair Altitude Sensor: notifies the pilot with visual and audio cues of critical altitude changes to avoid passing out from hypoxia. This remarkable system should be in every plane in the air either as a primary or secondary system.

Electroair Ignition System: the first-ever electronic ignition system with a unique sensor to be installed on a Piper Malibu Lycoming Engine by San Diego's High Performance Aircraft. By making engines more efficient and burn cleaner, less fuel is required and burned. Electroair's ignition system offers significant cost savings for any pilot flying a piston aircraft and is better for the environment.

MT-Propeller Composite 4-Bladed Propeller: This cutting-edge blade technology increases climb performance of the aircraft by two hundred to three hundred feet per minute, an important safety advantage in mountainous areas like San Diego. Surprisingly, this climb propeller also increases cruise speed by 2 to 3 knots. These increases allow planes to fly further and faster on the same amount of fuel thereby making aviation less expensive and more available to more people. The *Spirit of San Diego* was the first Piper Malibu Mirage in the United States to have this technology advantage.

FlightShield's Nanoceramic Coating: This state-of-the-art coating technology reduces drag over the wings and fuselage, which allows the plane to fly faster and farther on the same amount of fuel, lowering the hourly operating cost and making aviation more affordable for every pilot. If a pilot can get farther on every gallon of fuel there is a smaller carbon signature and this is better for the environment. FlightShield's coating is so slippery it prevents bugs and dirt from sticking to the aircraft, allowing for less frequent washing, which reduces the amount of water needed to keep the plane clean. 65 N River Lane Suite 201, Geneva, IL 60134, dzeitler@flightshield.com

Lightspeed PFX Noise Cancelling Headset: Being able to clearly hear what air traffic controllers, tower operators and other pilots are saying is a critical safety issue for pilots. The *Spirit of San Diego* showcases the PFX headset's acoustic response mapping, which uses microphones to measure your personal auditory landscape for the unique size and shape of your ear and fine-tune the noise cancelling and audio response.

Garmin Flight Stream 210: A small wireless gateway, Garmin's ground-breaking technology speeds the transfer of route information back and forth to the plane's onboard systems, which saves time and money while the engine is running. Installed by Neal Aviation, it allows a simple iPad to act as another synthetic vision flight display at a fraction of the normal cost, significantly increases cockpit safety and automation and reduces pilot workload. Seconds saved on the ground and in the air mean lower flight costs, greater safety and more fun, which draws younger pilots into aviation instead of to their video games!

AmSafe General Aviation Airbags: More than 95 percent of pilots survive a water landing, but often times they are knocked unconscious. The AmSafe general aviation airbags installed in the *Spirit of San Diego* at High Performance Aircraft in San Diego help to keep a pilot conscious during a water impact and are a significant safety improvement for any aircraft. I felt it was crucial to install these airbags to help ensure a safe escape from the plane should it go down over the Atlantic. Indian or Pacific Oceans.

DeLorme inReach Explorer by Garmin: This Satellite communication device allows you to send text messages, emails and post to social media in flight anywhere on the planet. It connects to your smart phone via Bluetooth for easy use. You can send an SOS for help, which gives your exact GPS position. It keeps you connected when off the gird and outside cell phone range. No pilot should fly without one.

Appendix Two

List of Sponsors

(alphabetical order)

Advanced Aircraft Service

Allison McCloskey Escrow Company

Alt Alert

Anderson Aviation Inc.

Ax Center for Experimental Cosmology (ACEC)

Best Western

Bill's Aircraft Service Inc.

BlacART Creative Group

BNC Bank

Callahan Thompson Sherman & Caudill LLP: CTSC Law

Cambridge Property Management

CAPS Training

CG Club Glove

Clean Wings Aviation

DeLorme

Electroair

Garden of Life

Garmin

General Aviation Support Egypt (GASE)

Gibbs

High Performance Aircraft

Landmark Aviation

Lightspeed Aviation

Lindbergh Schweitzer Elementary School

Live Fit Films-Phoebe Chongchua

Malaysia Airports

Malibu/Mirage Owners & Pilots Association (MMOPA)

Marv Golden Pilot Supplies

Mary Marcdante

MT-Propeller USA

Muns Law Firm

Neal Aviation

Online Promotion Success, Susan Gilbert

Oregon Aero

Passey-Bond Co.

Passport Health

Pilot Eyes

Pilot Getaways

Scheyden Precision Eyewear

SkyChick Adventures

Tahoe Truckee Airport

TEDx Talks

World Fuels

Support provided by:

Aircraft Owners and Pilots Association

Canadian Owners Pilots Association

Appendix Three

Countries Visited

St John's, Newfoundland

Santa Maria, Azores

Porto, Portugal

Gibraltar

Marrakech, Morocco

Valencia, Spain

Mallorca, Spain

Grenchen, Switzerland

Elba, Italy

Valletta, Malta

Istanbul, Turkey

Lesbos, Greece

Crete, Greece

Cairo, Egypt

Abu Dhabi, UAE

Doha, Qatar

Muscat, Oman

Nagpur, India

Kuala Lumpur, Malaysia

Jakarta, Indonesia

Darwin, Australia

Mackay, Australia

Brisbane, Australia

Noumea, New Caledonia

Pago Pago, American Samoa

Christmas Island, Kiribati

Honolulu, Hawaii

Monterey, CA

Truckee, CA

San Diego, CA

Appendix Four

Basic Trip Facts

Departure Date San Diego: May 18, 2015

Return Date San Diego: August 22, 2015

Duration of Trip: 3 months 8 Days

Countries Visited: 23

Distance Traveled: Approximately 26,000 miles

Aircraft: 1997 Piper Malibu Mirage

Aircraft Name: The Spirit of San Diego

Aircraft Range with 2 Ferry tanks: Approximately 2600nm in economy cruise

Aircraft Fuel Capacity with 2 Ferry Tanks: 315 gallons of Avgas

Charities Supported:

Aircraft Owners and Pilots Association Scholarship Fund by the name: "The Spirit of San Diego." Lindbergh Schweitzer Elementary School 4th Grade Classes

Wikipedia Pages:

https://en.wikipedia.org/wiki/Robert_DeLaurentis_(aviator)

https://en.wikipedia.org/wiki/List_of_circumnavigations

Website: http://www.flyingthrulife.com

Facebook: https://www.facebook.com/flyingthrulife

Facebook: https://www.facebook.com/Rdel66

Twitter: https://twitter.com/flyingthrulife

LinkedIn: https://www.linkedin.com/in/rdelaurentis

Instagram: https://www.instagram.com/flying_thru_life/

Google+: https://plus.google.com/111924564541586258714

YouTube: https://youtu.be/R1rvVGbBWrg

Acknowledgments

I would like to thank all the people that made this epic adventure possible. Such a massive undertaking is clearly the work of an entire team. No one individual could do this trip alone.

The "Flying Thru Life" team included Susan Gilbert, Eddie Gould, Mary Marcdante, Phoebe Chongchua, and Tony Manolatos. We worked like a well-oiled machine for six months prior to my departure and nearly a year after my return. We collectively accomplished more than we ever thought humanly possible given the resources of time and money that we had. We were successful bringing ourselves into alignment with our Purpose, Passion and Spirit. We removed the resistance that had blocked us and as a result we achieved great things as we were "Flying Thru Life" and flowing with the current of life.

There were so many inexplicable things that happened on this project that I would be foolish not to acknowledge Spirit for its part in all this. First when I decided to take two years off to do the trip, write three books, magazine articles, and lecture I did not know how to fund it all. It was at this point I began to have one financial windfall after another. I had three in two weeks that would pay for the entire trip and another eight in the next two months that made the entire project possible.

Secondly with respect to the actual trip, if you walk away from death once you are lucky. If you walk away from death twice you are very lucky. If you walk away from death more than seven times you need another explanation … and for me that was that this trip was guided for a purpose greater than me. I believe it was intended to inspire people to stretch their limits to live fuller lives free of unnecessary fear and worry. In short to show them how to dream impossibly big and then make it happen.

Deep gratitude to my sponsors who believed in me and my impossibly big dream and stepped up throughout this trip to help me bring innovation and safety in general aviation into mainstream awareness locally and globally.

And special thanks to Diane O'Connell and her team of editors for taking over 200 pages of single-spaced content and delicately weaving them into an eloquent, compelling, and inspiring story that will touch the hearts and souls of anyone who ever dreamed of flying. Diane held her ground under great pressure and in the process earned my respect and became one of my teachers.

And finally, I want to thank the more than two hundred thousand people that followed and supported me on social media, TV, radio and in the newspapers. Their loving encouragement, blessings, emails, texts, and phone calls kept me going when I thought I could not go any further. They inspired me as much as my trip inspired them. When the odds were heavily stacked against me and it would have been so much easier to give up, they gave me a reason to keep going.

About the Author

Robert DeLaurentis loves to fly and is passionate about helping people face their fears and live their impossibly big dreams. He is a successful real estate entrepreneur and investor, pilot, speaker, author and philanthropist. He has an undergraduate degree in accounting from the University of Southern California and an advanced graduate degree in Spiritual Psychology with an emphasis in Consciousness, Health and Healing from the University of Santa Monica. A Gulf War veteran, Robert served in the Navy for 14 years. After receiving his pilot's license in 2009, Robert has flown solo in his single engine Piper Malibu Mirage "The Spirit of San Diego" to more than 33 countries in the past five years and completed his first solo circumnavigation in August 2015 visiting 23 countries in 98 days.

Robert is the author of *Flying Thru Life: How to Grow Your Business and Relationships With Applied Spirituality*, which shows people how to find the resources to live their impossibly big dreams with grace and ease. His second book *Zen Pilot: Flight of Passion and the Journey Within* offers real-life adventures, both harrowing and inspiring, along with tips and advice including "Zen Moments," from his recent around-the-world trip during the summer of 2015.

Robert is a welcome speaker, aviation thought leader and media guest, available to speak to business groups, pilot organizations, personal and professional development conferences, non-profit fundraisers, schools, and youth groups. For more information on speaking engagements or media appearances, please contact him at

www.FlyingThruLife.com/contact.

Dear Reader

I hope you've enjoyed *Zen Pilot: Flight of Passion and the Journey Within*. Sharing this life-changing adventure with you makes the journey even more meaningful.

If you stayed in touch during my circumnavigation via social media or sent me words of encouragement, saying thank you is an understatement. You have no idea how important your feedback and support were in getting me through moments of fear and discouragement as well as expanding moments of awe and wonder. I am so grateful to you.

If you're new to our *Flying Thru Life* Community, welcome, and thank you for coming on board with *Zen Pilot*. There are more adventures awaiting all of us.

To keep those adventures coming and make sure I'm helping you live your impossibly big dreams, I'd love to hear from you. I want to know what you liked in *Zen Pilot*, what you loved, what you wish I'd written more of or what didn't resonate with you. Your feedback is important to me. You inspire me. You can write to me at Robert@FlyingThruLife.com, comment on my blog posts at my website www.FlyingThruLife.com and connect with me on any of my social media platforms including Facebook: facebook.com/FlyingThruLife or twitter.com/FlyingThruLife.

I'd like to ask a favor of you...

If you have ever tried to get an important idea, product, service or book out into the world in a big way, you know how important testimonials and reviews can be. Would you help me put *Zen Pilot* on the map and write a review on Amazon? Even just a sentence or two helps. Here is a link to the book on Amazon: http://bit.ly/ZenPilot.

Thank you so much for reading and reviewing *Zen Pilot*. Let's keep flying and creating impossibly big dreams together.

On the wings of safety and adventure,

Robert DeLaurentis

Author | Pilot | Speaker

45010706R00194

Made in the USA
Middletown, DE
12 May 2019